JOURNEY
GOD'S
into
PRESENCE

Patricia R. Johnson

Gazelle
P R E S S

ISBN 1-58169-143-2
For Worldwide Distribution
Printed in the U.S.A.

Gazelle Press
P.O. Box 191540 • Mobile, AL 36619
800-367-8203

Note: Many of the names in this book have been changed to protect the privacy of the individuals involved.

TABLE OF CONTENTS

DEDICATION

*This book is dedicated
to Hugh A. Johnson, Jr.*

ACKNOWLEDGMENTS

I can't possibly acknowledge everyone or every way that help has come to me with this project. But I would like to say a special thanks to:

My children, Stephen and Dara, your vibrant lives pushed me to the finish line of this book.

My parents, Charles and Janice Rattley, there are no adequate words for your unwavering support and faith in me. Thank you.

My brother and sisters, Charles, Donna and Kimberly, I am so blessed to be in the same family with you three.

My sister-in-law, Jennifer, we've come a long way. Thank you for your love and support of me and the children.

My pastors, Bishop Harry and Michele Jackson, it's because of your wisdom, love and example that I'm where I am today.

My friends, especially Donna Mazyck, thank you for being there always.

My Hope Christian Church family, I love you and appreciate you, thank you for loving me.

My agent, Keith Carroll, you made this book a reality. Thank you.

My publisher, I'm so appreciative to you for taking a chance and believing in this project.

To the Lord with whom it all begins and ends.

FOREWORD

Patricia Johnson's book, *Journey Into God's Presence*, is actually an "Ugly Duckling Turned Into Beautiful Swan" story. Step by step, she takes the reader from tragedy to triumph, from chaos to order, from selfishness to love. Difficult problems are transformed into stepping stones, which, in turn, lead to a life of fulfillment and purpose. Although this book is warm and engaging, it has a clear instructive element. It teaches the reader how to discover the presence of God and the will of God. The presence of God for Patricia is a signpost or road marker that leads us into the will of God. When she doesn't know what to do, she seeks God's presence. As she moves through life, God seems to use His presence like a spiritual Global Positioning System (GPS). Every time Patricia makes a wrong turn, the Lord recalculates and directs her back into His purposes.

How does this apply to us? We often feel like Hans Christian Anderson's ugly duckling. Although he believed himself to be an ugly duckling, he was, in fact, a beautiful swan. In the same way, fears and personal crises can blind us to our unique destiny. Similar to the early days of the duckling's life, we are deflated by the temporary reality of a life that does not live up to our expectations. We are tempted to feel ashamed, inferior or cheated. Instead of discovering a vision for our lives, we often struggle with mere survival. We cry out to God to make sense out of the chaos. Patricia Johnson does not minimize this struggle; instead, she explains it.

This book will help anyone who desires to grow in their walk with God. It is a must-read for men and women who feel that their lives have been suddenly thrown off track by tragedy, pain or adverse circumstances. Patricia's gripping narrative allows the reader to feel her pain and her victory. As the book progresses, Patricia also gives the reader pointers on how to overcome internal spiritual hurdles such as depression, lust, loneliness and a host of other temptations which beset us all. No matter how challenging your life may seem today, you can make it if you follow Patricia's lead into the presence of God.

—*Harry R. Jackson, Jr.*

INTRODUCTION

Not long ago a question was put to me: "How do you live a dynamic faith everyday?" The answer was at once complex and simple: by encountering the presence of God.

One might further ask, "How do you encounter the presence of God? Isn't God's presence already in us, in light of such scriptures as, 'For in Him we live, and move, and have our being'" (Acts 17:28). The answer is, Yes, His presence is in us, but we can also encounter the presence of God in a different way.

From a biblical perspective, we can speak of God's presence from both a general and a personal perspective. Psalm 139:7 makes it clear that God's presence is everywhere, as we see in David's cry, "Where shall I go from your spirit, or where shall I flee from your presence?" In this general sense, God's presence is everywhere. However, God's presence can be uniquely present, as His own reference to His presence revealed when He told Moses, "My presence shall go with you, and I will give you rest" (Exodus 33:14). We see the personal presence of Jesus in His words to the disciples that He would show Himself to those that love and obey His commands (John 14:21). His presence was a physical as well as spiritual revelation of who He was.

Today, we have the presence of Jesus in the form of the indwelling presence of the Holy Spirit. And just as

His presence affected all those who came into contact with Him 2,000 years ago, His presence affects all those who come into contact with Him today.

Something happens when we encounter God's presence—a divine intersection occurs. Our lives, with all our weaknesses, intersect with all of who God is, including His love, power, strength, faithfulness, mercy, goodness, wisdom, and holiness. The more we abide at this divine intersection, the stronger we become physically, spiritually, and emotionally. This is because an exchange takes place at this intersection that is spoken of in II Corinthians 3:18, "But we all with open face beholding as in a glass the glory of the Lord, are changed into the same image from glory to glory, even as by the Spirit of the Lord." At this divine intersection between our lives and God's glory, we may choose to yield our lives to Him. If we yield, then God's power undergirds the weaknesses in our lives, and we are able to overcome life's challenges.

There are many avenues to the presence of God: worship and praise are chief among them. Reading the Word of God is also a means of coming into His presence. The Holy Spirit will often illuminate His will and give guidance and comfort just through the reading of His Word. Prayer, a dialogue both spoken and unspoken, is unparalleled in its ability to bring us into the place where God's presence dwells.

My interest was piqued about the question of living a dynamic life because, as a teacher of prayer, I have noticed that often, no matter where we are on our spiritual journey with the Lord, the initial spark that started us on our way can die out over time if it is not continually stoked with the fuel of God's presence. Over time, the excitement and spiritual thirst that initially pulled us towards Christ fades until the pull towards Christ is not strong enough to counter the tug towards negative habits, behaviors, and mindsets that had perhaps always been a part of our lives. Consequently, we find ourselves in a slow and sometimes rapid descent into former sin patterns, apathy, or even unbelief. When this happens, we not only become impotent in our ability to overcome life's challenges, but we are also frustrated in our efforts to fulfill the God-given purpose of our lives.

But this doesn't have to happen. Psalm 16:11a provides the answer, "You will show me the path of life: in thy presence is fulness of joy...." Encountering God's presence will illuminate the path of life that He has prepared for each of us and brings us the fulness of joy that we long for in our lives.

This book is the outgrowth of a 15-year journey that includes a path strewn with the debris of self-defeating mindsets. It is a journey launched by trauma and sustained by grace.

I wrote this book for those who, like me, want to know the "hows"—how did I overcome my fear; how did I get over my hurt; and how did I maintain peace in the midst of the storm? This book answers those questions, but not from the traditional self-help perspective. Instead, this book reads as an unfolding story that spans 15 crucial years of intense spiritual and emotional growth in my life. Intertwined throughout the story are relevant biblical principles that gave me direction, guidance, and hope.

It is my hope that light will be shed on the spiritual, emotional, and physical processes we all must experience if we desire our lives to reflect God's love, wisdom, and power.

For me, the journey has not always been pleasant, nor have the lessons been swift. I've learned that if we are willing, we will find that God's presence will not just lead us through the circumstances, but as we learn to seek, discern, and dwell in God's presence, we will safely land where we need to be. For me, that place is called destiny.

Chapter 1

When Things
Don't Go as Planned

On the shores of darkness there is light
And precipices show untrodden green,
There is a budding morrow in midnight,
There is a triple sight in blindness keen.
—Homer

The day that would change all the rest of my days began with a simple telephone call. Sarah, Congressman Mickey Leland's secretary, was on the phone. She was calling to tell me not to worry, but that the plane transporting Mickey, my husband Hugh, and 14 others hadn't reached its destination.

"They probably missed a connection. It's happened before," she stated with ease. "It's just that the press has gotten wind of it, so I wanted to let you know before you saw it on television." Her voice, though even-toned, sounded rehearsed. Instinctively, the air caught in my

1

throat, and I thanked her for calling, trying to reciprocate the attitude of unfeigned calm I sensed she was trying hard to convey. *"Hugh, where are you?"* I called out, my voice barely above a whisper, my heart still pounding from the impact of Sarah's words.

It was almost noon when that call had come. I had just gone into the kitchen to fix something for lunch when the phone rang. Stephen, our two-year-old son, and Dara, our daughter who was just about to reach her six-month milestone, had finally settled down for their afternoon naps. Looking around our kitchen—still a patchwork of our latest renovation efforts—I placed the phone back in its cradle on the freshly painted pale yellow wall, catching just briefly the faint scent of wood from the newly installed kitchen cabinets. Everything was still except for the slight creak of plywood beneath my feet.

Hugh, where are you? I asked again, this time silently. Sitting down in a kitchen chair near the phone, I took a deep breath and then exhaled. Letting the air out slowly, my eyes took in the new and the old of our evolving kitchen; the newly painted walls, and the rough plywood floor; the soft, burnished luster of the new cabinets over the decades old porcelain sink speckled with rust; the creaky, wooden frame door that opened to the backyard that for now was overgrown with weeds. In time, it was to be a place of play and rest. I was seeing but not seeing, just hoping against hope that this time tomorrow everything would still be the same.

Our house was a fixer-upper, located on a quiet city street, lined with trees of maple and oak. The pale green, wooden frame, turn of the century house with its sagging wrap-around porch had immediately caught our eyes as we surveyed the modest mix-match of clapboard, brick, and wooden houses that flanked this neighborhood street. It stood out on a street that, to me, was vintage D.C., where large towering oaks embraced from opposite sides of the street in a tangled arch of branches and leaves that shimmered deep green in the spring and bold red and brilliant yellow in the fall.

We spied our jewel in the rough a few months before we were married, marveling at our good fortune in finding a house that needed just enough work to make it affordable, while possessing enough old house charm to make it worth the effort to buy. Hugh relished the task of plastering, painting, stripping floors, finding out-dated fixtures and enduring my light-hearted teasing that he was living out a repressed ambition to be an architect.

A few months after we were married I became pregnant with our son Stephen, and before Stephen was a year old, Dara was on the way. Soon the desire to fix up the house became a mission spurred on by the need to make the place safe and habitable for our children. *Hugh, you have to come home and finish fixing up this place,* I thought. *I need you.* "But not just to fix the house," I pointedly said aloud, sorry that I had even made a connection in my mind between his absence and working on this house. *This job was supposed to be a blessing,* I lamented. But now I was having serious doubts, my emotions vacillating between anger and dread.

Mickey Leland, known as a maverick Congressman

from Texas, was co-founder of the Select Committee on Hunger. He had offered Hugh the job as a professional staff member and head of the Committee's international team a few short months ago. The two met after Alison Leland, Mickey's wife and a good friend of mine from college, had called Hugh to ask him if he was interested in the job. She knew, through conversations with me, that Hugh knew something about international policy and development from his days as a lawyer in a firm in Brazil. Hugh's current job was professionally satisfying most of the time, but it really didn't fulfill his passion to work on international development issues. So we were both happy when Mickey called after their meeting to offer him the job, and Alison and I were thrilled at the prospect of our husbands working together, imagining shared trips, intense meetings, and a long life of friendship fueled by the intertwining of our lives.

There was no further word on their whereabouts that day or the next. Soon the craziness began, like some sort of videotape spinning wildly out of control. First, it was the incessant barrage of knocks on my front door; knocks that made my blood run cold because they symbolized more than just polite requests for interviews by the press. For me, they were the beaks of vultures tap, tap, tapping at their prey, trying to determine if any life was still left in my husband or perhaps in me—it was hard to say. And though they were only doing their job, trying to get the hot story, their mere presence was a reminder that my husband was not home. He was out there somewhere in Ethiopia, hopefully still on a mission to determine the state of hunger in refugee camps. At least that was the thought I tried hard to hold onto.

The days ticked by. I consoled myself with the thought that if he were dead, I'd know it. I was certain that I'd feel it. As the week wore on, it became harder and harder to do anything except nod as conversations drifted by. I was present, but not present. I was trying to picture Hugh in Ethiopia. I was trying to picture him before he left. And most of the time I was just trying to get through the next moment in a seamless stretch of days that had become excruciating.

The screen door that let out to our front porch screeched perpetually, and I wondered how long its fragile frame would hold up under what seemed to be an endless stream of people. For one whole week family and friends and even strangers gathered together from sun up to sun down to offer hope to me and to one another in the form of a possibility here, a different perspective there, with one thing in common: all were glued by a bond of pain that held us together, tighter and tighter, day after day, squeezing out the cacophonous void of "No news yet," with the empty, yet comforting refrain, "It's going to be okay."

I guess this is our fifteen minutes of fame, Hugh? I joked with a weak laugh to myself one day when the news reports that filtered up to my bedroom were particularly copious. And then the call came at about one a.m. as I lay in bed, real sleep continuing to elude me. It was Sarah again. They'd found the plane, but the rescuers hadn't made it to the site yet. "Hold on," she said. "I'm calling as a heads up. They don't know what they'll

5

find." At five a.m., call number two came. This time my father answered the phone. They were on site at the base of a mountain.

"No survivors," my father faintly whispered as he slowly put the receiver down. The words assaulted my ears, echoing with a clarity that would not allow me the gift of ignorance. The waiting was over. My husband was dead.

I needed air. Leaving my children with my parents, I got in the car and headed for Rock Creek Park, a place where the dense woods and infrequent pedestrian traffic would hopefully provide the solitude I needed. Moving through the streets of D.C., I made my way around the curving streets of the park. With a feeble sense of victory, I located a place where I could sit unnoticed by the rocky crevices that dotted the winding, sparkling waters of the creek. Water had always been so soothing to me, especially when I was depressed, but I knew I needed more than the soothing calm of this rocky creek.

Lord I need you, came the silent demand from my soul.

God Is Comfort

God's presence not only brings comfort, but God *is* comfort. In the early days of the Church, the disciples knew the presence of Jesus in the flesh while he resided on earth. They were upset about the prospect of Jesus leaving them, a fact that He told them would take place as a result of His crucifixion. However, Jesus also told them that just because He was leaving didn't mean that they would be alone. When He left, another, like Himself would come to be present with them. "Nevertheless I tell you the truth; it is expedient for you that I go away: for if I go not away, the Comforter will not come unto you; but if I depart, I will send him unto you" (John 16:7). The comforter was and is the Holy Spirit. The Greek word for Comforter is *paraklete*. It not only means comforter, but also advocate and helper. As *paraklete*, the Holy Spirit not only comes to comfort us when needed, but also to help us by making God's spiritual resources available to us in the way that we need so that we can live our lives as God intended.

In the case of trauma or tragedy, the Holy Spirit is there to comfort, but His comfort does not necessarily replace the grieving process. Rather, He helps us to go through circumstances without the irreparable pain and emotional scarring that could result without His help. We see God's desire to comfort us in the words of Isaiah, "As one whom his mother comforts so will I comfort you…" (Isaiah 66:10-13). Unfortunately, sometimes, our immediate pain and anger can hinder us from receiving the full extent of God's comfort. We must then grow in our understanding and our ability to receive the gift of comfort that God desires to extend.

There in the car beside the creek, tears began to fill my eyes, burning my lids, and blurring my vision, and I gave myself permission to cry. I had barely cried during the entire previous week, believing in some confused way that my tears would in some way confirm what my heart refused to believe—that Hugh was gone. And so, consciously or unconsciously, I finally gave myself permission to open the floodgates of my soul, and released what felt like a river of tears that had been stored up like a dam as a surety against this encroaching nightmare.

Chapter 1: Study Questions

Have you ever experienced a sudden trauma or significant disappointment in your life? If so, how did you deal with it?

What are your thoughts about God's sovereignty in our lives?

How do you react when sudden trauma or destruction occurs in your world? Do you turn towards God or away? Why?

JFK & MLK
- death of fiancé
- nephew's death
- divorce
- mother's death

Chapter 2

Our Extremity,
God's Opportunity

As a man thinks of himself, so he is...(Proverbs
23:7).

The drive back home from Andrews Air Force
Base was quiet. Mom, Dad, and Daddy J were all
seated stiffly in the rear seat of the blue
Suburban, seemingly lost in their own private worlds of
remembering. Our military escorts, the driver and an of-
ficer in the front passenger seat, rode along silently,
doing their best to convey the right note of somber sen-
sitivity in light of the occasion. Two weeks had passed
since the news of the crash, and now Hugh, Mickey, and
the twelve other Americans on the plane were finally
home. Standing on the tarmac, watching the soldiers un-
load their caskets one by one from the gaping mouth of
the large cargo plane, an ironic hint of a smile formed
somewhere deep inside. *How wonderful*, I thought to
myself, *that Hugh at least had a job that he loved.*

He had confided in me shortly before he left for Ethiopia that this was the best job he had ever had. He had waxed on and on, more animated than his usual laid-back self, about how this job had exposed him to things he never would have dreamed of experiencing in his lifetime, from maneuvering to get a bill through Congress that would provide food for millions to riding in a military-led motorcade through the streets of Addis Ababa. I wondered, *Was worth it? Had he completed his mission in life? Was God giving him a grand send off?* And although, for a brief instant, a smile had formed deep within, this was no laughing matter. Hugh and fifteen others, including the two Ethiopian pilots, were gone, cut down in the primes of their lives. *Was there a reason for such tragedy? For any tragedy?*

And then as immaculate soldiers ever so meticulously folded the American flags from each coffin and marched lock-step to the collective heartbeat of the families present, the words gently, but surely, resounded silently in my head, *"Unless a grain of wheat falls into the ground and dies, it remains alone, but if it dies, it bears much fruit."*

Was that you, Lord? Are you trying to tell me something with that scripture? The media attention had focused the world's radar screen on the problem of hunger. Perhaps thousands of lives would be saved because of Mickey's legacy in Congress and the outpouring of goodwill to honor the memory of the lives of those on the plane. *Was this the fruit you are talking about?* I silently questioned. Perhaps. Or perhaps it was that and something more? Maybe something more personal to

10

my life? I positioned my head closer to the window pane, cool from the steady blast of the air conditioner, a stark contrast to the withering August heat outside. I thought not only about what might lie ahead, but what had gone before.

Staring blankly out of the tinted window, my eyes took in the muted sunlight that cast a surreal pall over the busy D.C. streets that whizzed by. As they did, I went back, sifting through the memories, sorting through the moments of our life together like a string of tangled beads.

Sick and Tired of Being Sick and Tired

So much had changed in such a short time. I had been in my last year of law school when I first met Hugh. The idea that it was either now or never and that I was either going to succeed and fulfill my potential or not had been resonating like a clanging gong in the back of my mind for months. When was I going to be the "real" person I knew existed inside? When was I going to be happy in a relationship and finally take off the make-believe coat of "It'll get better" that I was wearing again in my current relationship? When was I going to put all of my efforts into experiencing the kind of success I knew I was capable of achieving?

As these questions swirled within my head, a growing sense of urgency to free myself from the internal and external stagnation caused by my lifestyle began to accumulate. *Change* was my daily mantra and it seemed to sound loudest in the area of relationships.

Of the "serious" relationships in which I'd been a

participant, all, I lamented sadly, had been missing some key elements of emotional or intellectual connectedness. But sadder still was the fact that I had stayed in some of these relationships long after the bell should have tolled. Louis was no exception.

Louis wasn't a bad guy by any standards, and I did care for him. Smart and good looking, an engineer by profession, he had been a good companion, filling my days and nights with conversation and comfort, the kind of comfort that—when the music was right and the lights were low—might be mistaken for love. But it wasn't love, no matter how much I tried to convince myself otherwise. He professed to love me, but the passionless look in his eyes always seemed to belie his words. Sometimes I thought he was just too tired to look any further. Sometimes I thought I was too. So we just stayed in the relationship.

Why had I stayed with him, I asked myself? Fear, I suppose. I wasn't getting any younger. Besides, many people told me I should be grateful to have even found him, much less think about leaving him. The problem was there was no life in me when I was with him, and I found myself increasingly engaged in a sort of mental pep talk whenever we planned to get together.

And then there was law school. "Just keep a step or two behind the threshold of excellence," seemed to be my unspoken motto. I had recently come to the unpleasant conclusion that the reason for this proclivity towards mediocrity was that if I stepped over the threshold of excellence and actually succeeded at what I was doing, on a *consistent* and *noticeable level,* then I'd have to live up to a reputation that my sense of self wasn't sure I was capable of maintaining.

I was certain that my relationship with Louis and mediocrity were both linked together. To stay relatively positive, I lived in the future—whether consciously or subconsciously, I'm not sure. And in my moments of truth, I wore what I cynically described to myself as my make-believe coat of "It'll get better." This was a coat that I'd found served its purpose well by covering any voids in my life, be they in relationships or in school or anywhere else I was afraid to extend myself. My rationale, I surmised, was probably something like, *since things were going to improve one day, there was no need to worry about the present.* But the internal pressure was building and the coat was getting ragged. During that period in my life, whenever I looked in the mirror, I reminded myself of a broken mirror, all the pieces cracked and distorted, yet somehow reflecting me.

As we continued on the drive home from Andrews Air Force Base, the drone of the engine and the silence of the passengers coaxed me into deeper reflection. With four years of hindsight I could see now that the Holy Spirit had been stirring the waters of healing for me, just as the angel had stirred the water for the man at the pool of Bethesda 2000 years previously.

God's Presence Heals

Jesus asked the infirm man at the pool of Bethesda, "Do you want to be made well?" (John 5:6) The man had many excuses as to why he couldn't get down into the water when the angel stirred the pool and healing flowed to all who got in. The man had been infirm for 38 years. I, too, had been infirm for a very long time.

Looking back at that time in my life, I could see that the build up of my internal frustration was the Holy Spirit's way of stirring the waters of healing for me. It wasn't, I recalled, until my internal level of frustration with Louis, school, and ultimately with myself had exceeded my ability to cope that I was willing to make a change. I was reminded of the concept that God often allows us to come to the end of our self-efforts so that we will turn to Him because only in turning to Him will we find true meaning and purpose in our lives.

In the words of noted teacher Jack Frost of Shiloh Place Ministries, "You must *hurt* enough that you have *no choice* but to change." That had definitely been true of me, I thought to myself with a slight smirk. It was also true that my actions and negative thought patterns were the product of my fear of change and self-doubt. The fear of leaving the safe confines of the relationship with Louis and the self-doubt about my abilities were strongholds that had built up in my mind over the years. These strongholds had kept me in the same pattern of low expectations, both in school and in relationships.

In Jack Frost's series entitled "Bitter-root Strongholds," a stronghold is defined as:

A habit-structure of thought that we have embraced at the core of our inner being. It is built upon a foundation of lies and half-truths. It has become a fortress of thought that influences the way we respond to the truth about God's character within us.

Proverbs 23:7 says, "For as he thinks within himself, so he is." This means that whatever you believe about yourself becomes the truth, whether it is true in reality or not.

What lies had I turned into truth? I wondered. Was it the insensitive words of a teacher that equated to "You're not smart enough," or the unkind taunts of bullies which told me, "Those kids are saying those things because there's something wrong with you."

Negative thought patterns enter our minds from many sources. Emotional and physical abuse from parents or others in authority are often initial gateways to negative thought patterns. Such abuse can include negative words spoken about one's abilities, emotional neglect, extreme authoritarianism or passivism by a parent, or physical and sexual abuse. Other, perhaps more overlooked, sources of negative thought patterns include a performance-oriented home where there is no room for failure, the lack of expressed love and affection either in the home or by other affirming sources, and rejection by peers (Frost, 1998).

This list of the sources for negative thought patterns is not exhaustive by any means, but it does highlight significant entry points. If these negative thought patterns are not dealt with, eventually an emotional and spiritual stronghold is built. In my case, a stronghold of fear and self-doubt, of not measuring up, and of not deserving better was allowed free reign to develop.

Healing Waters

The pool of water stirred by the angel in the scripture can be likened to the healing from the Holy Spirit that we can experience today. The Bible says living water flows from the throne of heaven (Rev. 7:17; Rev. 22:2). Living water is often symbolic in the Bible of the life of God:

> *And it shall come to pass that everything that lives, which moves, wherever the river comes, shall live...because these waters shall come toward: for they shall be healed and everything shall live where the river comes"* (Ezekiel 47:9).

As the Holy Spirit pours living water upon our souls, a stirring occurs deep within. The Psalmist says it this way, "Deep calleth unto deep at the noise of thy waterspouts: all thy waves and thy billows are gone over me" (Psalm 44:7). The stirring of the Holy Spirit agitates the strongholds that have accumulated over time in our souls. The more He pours, the greater the stir within, and the greater the sense of internal pressure. Hurts, wounds, long-standing areas of unforgiveness, along with other strongholds that may have long been buried begin to rise to the surface of our consciousness. There's no reason to fear or retreat from this process. The Holy Spirit knows when and how much to pour and how much stirring we can take. He pours because the question Jesus asked the man at the pool of Bethesda is still valid today: "Do you want to be healed?"

Just like the man at the pool, I had a choice. I could have held on to my excuses and continued on a path of sure defeat; but God, in His compassion, didn't allow me the luxury of my excuses, just as He didn't allow them for the infirm man. *Wow*, I thought to myself, remembering this time in my life as if it were yesterday. The memory of my decision washed over me like a wave.

With all the bravado I could muster at the time, I had called Louis up and told him it was over. He didn't believe me at first, as I knew he wouldn't. "You've sung this tune before," he had said mockingly, his tone reverberating in my mind even now. He had been right. I usually did go back to him. At the time I couldn't articulate to him why this time was different and didn't have the energy to try. I knew in my heart it was over, and that was all that mattered. Although I didn't feel like anything earth shattering had happened, I knew it had. I had climbed over a significant border of fear and self-doubt that, for so long, had quenched the life flow of my potential.

Thinking back, yielding was the key to my decision at the time. With Louis, I had to be willing to yield my fear of not getting married or of even having a relationship, and I had to yield my mind to a new way of thinking and press through the barriers of self-doubt and low self-expectations. It was no accident, I mused, that a few weeks after closing the door to Louis, a new door opened bringing Hugh into my life.

17

He Gives Good Gifts

Hugh and I were standing in the church's narrow vestibule, in a line of people waiting to go into the sanctuary at my cousin's wedding. We had met ten years previously in college. He had been a senior at Morehouse College, and I had been a freshman at Spelman, its sister school. Back then we had only been casual acquaintances. He soon graduated and that was the last I saw of him until this wedding we both were attending. He was standing a few people behind me, and as I turned around to survey the crowd, I caught a glimpse of him catching a glimpse of me. He stood out at about six foot two, his broad shoulders ensconced in a nicely fitted dark blue suit. He had friendly eyes and a warm smile, and his slightly receding hairline made him look just a little older than his years, which I estimated to be about 30.

We recognized each other immediately, even though it had been years since we had last seen one another. Later on at the reception, I found out that he was a lawyer, having graduated from Columbia Law School a few years back, a fact that I thought was such a coincidence since I was in my third year of law school at Howard University and anxiously waiting to join his ranks.

We exchanged numbers that night. As we got to know one another, I began to realize that the Hugh I was getting to know now was not the same Hugh I had known even casually in college. It wasn't just that ten years had passed. One day Hugh shared with me that a few years back he had made a decision to become a

18

Christian. Outwardly, he related, there was nothing dramatic about this decision, however, internally he believed the changes were profound. He told me he no longer felt as if he was just out there in life wondering what his next step would or should be. He felt anchored and guided by a love that was hard to comprehend. Listening to him at the time made me want to know this God—this Christ—that seemed so real to Hugh.

I had grown up believing in God, but He had never been an up close and personal part of my life the way He seemed to be in Hugh's. However, in recent years, as a burgeoning twenty-something professional, I had begun to think more about issues of faith. So, when Hugh began to tell me about his faith, I was perhaps more ready to listen than I been in years. What I didn't understand at the time was that not only was I listening to Hugh, but I was also experiencing God's presence.

His Draws Us to His Presence Through People

People are the containers of God's presence. Jesus confirms this when He says,

> *If a man love me, he will keep my words: and my Father will love him, and we will come unto to him and make our abode with him* (John 14:23).

It is the presence of God in individuals that is often the initial gateway that beckons us to experience the love of Christ for ourselves.

God's presence is most often expressed through love;

"By this shall all men know that you are my disciples, if you love one another" (John 13:35). His presence is also revealed in the form of His power manifested in an individual's life, as stated by Paul, "But we have this treasure in earthen vessels, that the excellency of the power may be of God, and not of us" (2 Corinthians 4:7).

I could see now how clearly these principles were in operation when I met Hugh. Looking at Hugh's life and the peace and stability he exuded—which he attributed to his relationship with Christ—intensified my desire to be closer to God. I began to pray for answers to the questions I had about God, about faith, about Christ.

With an increasingly tender heart and Hugh's gentle encouragement, I had found that my faith in Christ began to grow. And although my faith was fledgling, the benefits I received from my growing relationship with Christ were not. This was especially so when I prayed. In prayer my spirit felt cradled, nourished, and strengthened by a peace that I could not manufacture on my own.

I sighed, reluctantly coming back to the present. Yes, so much has happened. As the blue Suburban pulled up to our house, the same house that two weeks ago Hugh and I had shared together, I silently prayed that God would flood my heart with that same peace right now.

Chapter 2: Study Questions

Seldom - try to stay optimistic

To what extent do you see evidence of negative thought patterns in your life? If so, what do you believe are the sources of these patterns? *- hurt of love - rejection*

Have you ever felt an internal pressure to change your actions or thoughts? If so, what did it feel like, and how did you respond? *Peace Corp*

Have you met anyone whose life strongly seemed to reflect the spirit of Christ? If so, what were the characteristics you noticed?

Are there areas in your life where Christ could be reflected more clearly?

- forgiveness

Fruits of the Spirit
- patience
- love
- joy
- kindness
- goodness
- faithfulness
- gentleness
- self-control

Chapter 3

God, Are You Real?

Every day since the crash, I had awakened to what could only be described as a cloud of depression that seemed to literally engulf me as soon as my eyes sensed light and my mind registered anew that Hugh was gone. Its presence was palpable, sapping my energy and clouding my thoughts. It didn't help that the old furnace needed to be replaced, plumbing work had to be done, and Stephen had to go to the emergency room for an asthma attack. The needs column was piling up. The emotional resources column was at zero. To cope I went into autopilot. Do whatever is necessary, don't think too much, don't cry too much, just get through it. This worked fine for a few months until I realized there was something else going on inside besides emotional and physical exhaustion. I was angry—angry with God and even angry with Hugh. Why was this happening? *Where were you, God?* Even more searing was the question: How could a loving God allow my husband to die at such a young age, leaving two small children and a young wife?

As much as I tried not to admit it, Hugh's death had ripped a huge hole in the security blanket of my faith. It had caused me to question just how sovereign God was in our lives anyway. After all, I had prayed Psalm 91:9-10 before Hugh left, "Because you have made the Lord who is my refuge, even the Most High, your dwelling place, no evil shall befall you, nor shall any plague come near your dwelling."

Hadn't Hugh made the Lord his dwelling place? Well, as far as I was concerned, evil certainly seemed to have befallen him at least so far as the ending of his physical life. *What happened God? Where were you?*

No More Hallelujahs!

When Hugh died, I decided not to return to the church we had attended as a couple, simply for the reason that when I had married Hugh I had married his church. We were no longer married, and as far as I was concerned, my obligation to attend the church was over. There wasn't anything wrong with the church or its members. Perhaps it was the fact that the majority of the people were much older than I, and there were very few children my own children's ages. As my children grew older, I wanted a place where they would feel comfortable as well. I had been a Christian for three years and still felt relatively new at this church-going business. Nevertheless, new or not, I did believe that church had an important role to play in my spiritual development. It was intended to be a place where one's faith was bolstered through teaching and nurturing relationships. For me, regardless of my anger at God, it was a place where I also hoped to shore up the gaps in my beleaguered spiritual armor.

With the goal in mind of putting down new spiritual roots, I packed Stephen, Dara, their car seats, diaper bags and double-stroller into the car and set out to attend yet another service that might prove to be the one we could call home. Yet even as I walked through another set of doors, a smile plastered on my face and the ever ready spiritual epithet tumbling from my lips, questions assailed my mind. *Why are you here, what good will it do?* Usually about halfway through the service, as the tempo got faster, the hands rose higher and the preacher got louder, I would get up and leave in frustration, anger, and bewilderment. *How could people praise God the way they do in the face of such tragedy and destruction in the world? How could I praise a God whom I wasn't sure if I could even trust?*

Things finally came to a head one particular Sunday morning. I was sitting in the middle of a long row of people in a church that I had harbored hopes might be the one we would attend regularly. The fervor of the pastor and the volume of the music were particularly irksome to me that Sunday with no end in sight. All of a sudden I felt as if was going to explode! *If that pastor says "Hallelujah, thank you, Jesus," one more time, I'm going to scream. Thank you, Jesus, for what? The death of my husband?*

Unceremoniously, and without regard for the ten sets of legs I had to squeeze through to get out, I picked up Stephen in one arm and Dara in the other and, ignoring piercing stares, marched up the aisle. Upon reaching the massive exit doors, I met the usher's glare eye for eye and dared her to say something to me. *Did she think I didn't know I was creating a scene? Move out of the way,* was the message my eyes spoke for my lips. She reluctantly opened the massive doors, and I walked out into the bright noonday sun.

Stephen and Dara might have been young, but they knew when mommy was upset. Dara began to cry as I strapped her into her seat, and Stephen returned my gaze with a look of bewilderment. "It's okay, Stephen and Dara, Mommy is just sad, like you get sad sometimes. I miss Daddy. Don't worry. Let's go get some ice cream," I said brightly, knowing I was probably playing out what not to do in the grieving process.

As I steered the car towards the ice cream shop, I silently began a conversation: *God, you have got to help me. I can't keep doing this. It's not good for my children or for me. I believe You exist. You seemed so real to me just a few months ago. Why didn't You stop the plane from going into the mountain? You are really going to have to help me to believe that You're in control.*

I knew that I had to make a decision. I couldn't go on like this, running from church to church. I felt like a person in a desert, finally reaching a glistening body of water only to find sand dripping from their lips. I knew myself. Sooner or later I would stop searching all together. *And then where would I be?*

His Presence Is a Choice

When we do not understand why something has happened, does it mean that God is not in control? Often, that is the unfortunate conclusion we make. Faith is a belief that something exists when there is no tangible evidence of its reality, as stated in Hebrews 11:1. "Now faith is the substance of things hoped for, the evidence of things not seen." Faith in Christ is no guarantee that we will not face problems. In fact, Jesus reminded His disciples,

These things I have spoken to you, that in Me you may have peace. In the world you will have tribulation, but be of good cheer, I have overcome the world (John 16:33).

Often we assume that our faith is a guarantee that life will be problem free, but this is not what the Bible teaches. It does promise that we will have access to the resources of heaven to face and overcome whatever comes our way, and yes, at times even avoid many of life's challenges. However, the following words of Peter for the church are just as true today as they were when he exhorted the readers of his letter to remain strong in the midst of trials and to even rejoice in the midst of the season of adversities.

That the trial of your faith, being much more precious than of gold that perishes, though it be tried with fire, might be found unto praise and honor and glory at the appearing of Jesus Christ (I Peter 1:6-7).

But how are we to rejoice when things seem so out of control and painful at times? First, we must understand that our faith is a choice. We can choose to believe what He says in His Word about who He is, or we can choose not to believe. One of the things God says about Himself is that He does not change, "With whom is no variableness, neither shadow of turning" (James 1:17). When our faith is weakened, one of the ways to strengthen it and hold onto what we know about God is to go back and remind ourselves about the times God was real to us, and our faith was strong. When David was greatly distressed, he encouraged himself in the Lord his God (I Samuel 30:6). Jehoshaphat too made a declaration of God's might and power when he was about to fight what looked like an unwinnable war (II Chronicles 20:6-7).

Turn Towards Him

I concluded that I wasn't to the point where I could rejoice as Peter exhorted us to do, but I knew my faith was a choice. I had to choose to continue believing even in the face of my hurt and uncertainty, putting my faith in Christ's promise that He who had overcome the world would make a way for me to overcome my current tribulation. I began to remind myself of what God had done for me, such as when Stephen recently went to the emergency room with an asthma attack and my prayers had been accompanied by an internal reassurance that he would be okay.

Slowly, the slightest slivers of light began to shine their way into the darkness that had inched its way over my soul. *We are always so quick to blame you for our pain,* I thought apologetically, *when in fact you told us who to blame:*

> *The thief cometh not, but for to steal, and to kill and to destroy: I am come that they might have life, and that they might have it more abundantly* (John 10:10).

This world was not what God had originally intended it to be, I lamented, a rising tide of clarity beginning to overcome my earlier despair. I realized that the schemes of the enemy of our souls, and our own errors and sins leave us vulnerable to all kinds of havoc and pain. I didn't know why God had allowed Hugh to die, but I finally came to a stark conclusion. I had a choice—either allow anger and unbelief to get a grip on my emotions or choose to trust that God had not changed from the loving God I believed Him to be before Hugh died and that He would be there for me in the days ahead.

① Mother's death

Chapter 3: Study Questions

Have you ever experienced a time in your life when you questioned God's love for you? If so, how do feel about his love for you now?

Think of two significant times in your life when you knew God was real in your life. What were the circumstances? How did you know God was real?

What process do you go through internally to build yourself back up in your faith?

→ Shortly after divorce
– stressed to max

– Ghana (snake)

– financial struggle following divorce
– job making 2x salary

Chapter 4

Making Sure It's God's Direction

Courage is not the absence of fear,
But rather the judgment that something else
Is more important.
                    —Ambrose Redmoon

To Be or Not To Be

God stirs the waters in many ways. Sometimes the waters bring healing; sometimes they bring windows of opportunities. Once again, the door is opened, and the way is clear for us to advance. The question then becomes, "Will you walk through the door?" "Why would you ever hesitate?" comes the reply. The answer: "Because you do not know what is on the other side of the door."

A month or so after the mad dash from the sanctuary, I received a call. It was from Marty, one of Hugh's colleagues on the Select Committee on Hunger. During the conversation, I mentioned to Marty that I planned to look for another job. At the time I was working for the

29

City Government, and although I liked my position, my real interest was similar to what Hugh had been working on: international development. Marty's response to my prospective job search was so quick and to the point, it was as if he had been thinking about his words for some time and was now seizing the opportunity to bring the discussion up with me.

"Why don't you apply for a job on the Hunger Committee?" he asked. "I know it sounds strange, but you are qualified and you should think about it, especially since you're thinking about looking for another job."

"Come on, Marty, you've got to be kidding," was my immediate reply. *I couldn't even consider such a thing,* I thought to myself. "Marty, I don't even want to look at the Capitol right now because it reminds me so much of Hugh, much less work in the same office."

Marty, however, was a persuasive talker and was not to be put off. He was a few years older than me, well respected on Capitol Hill and had worked for a number of influential politicians over the years. He had decided to retire from working full-time on the Hill in the policy arena, to pursue his passion for photography. In the short time that I had known Marty, I realized quickly that to know him was to love him. He was short in physical stature, but large on personality and had the kind of hearty and engaging laugh that melted pretenses in everyone from the most powerful to the average Joe. Marty was also a champion for the needs of others. And so, shortly after the crash, he had taken on the self-appointed role of protector for my children and me.

Marty had only known Hugh for the six months Hugh had worked on the Committee and yet had grown really fond of Hugh in that short time. He admired Hugh's keen intelligence and his love for his family. With tears in his eyes, he had related to me how he had come to know my husband on the first trip Hugh had taken to Ethiopia. Marty told me about the long flight and the way he and Hugh had laughed and exchanged their life stories as the long flight droned across the Atlantic. What had impressed Marty was the way Hugh had talked about me and the children, showing him pictures and lamenting about the fact that he had to be away from us because it meant leaving so soon after the birth of his month old daughter. So, perhaps out of a sense of duty, grief, and or paternal instinct, the children and I had become Marty's project. And he was determined to make sure that we landed on our feet. I suspected his suggestion to work on the Committee was not some idle whim either, but rather a well-thought-out analysis of the needs of both the Committee and me. Although he was sensitive to my feelings, he believed that, in light of my academic and professional background, my desire to get back into the international arena, I should at least consider the possibility of applying for a job on the Committee.

Marty continued in his best persuasive manner, "The Committee works on a variety of international policy issues, and you told me yourself that you liked the work that Hugh was doing."

I had liked the work Hugh was doing on the Committee and was always looking over his shoulder, putting in my two cents worth during those late nights when he pored through international policy briefs at the kitchen table. But could I join the Committee after my husband had died while working there? That seemed a bit farfetched, and it just didn't seem right for some reason.

"Marty, I have two babies, not to mention that I am a single parent. Working on the Hill is not going to be a picnic no matter how prestigious it's made out to be." I knew this first hand from Hugh's experience. "There are going to be many late nights and maybe a lot of travel time. I'm not sure I can handle the hours with the kids." I didn't mention the other thought that quickly skirted through my mind: The job would call for a great deal of public speaking, if the responsibilities were similar to Hugh's. Public speaking was something I was horribly afraid of. Law school had not cured me of this life-long fear, and I suspected no miracle was waiting in the wings. Marty continued to lay out the advantages, and heard me out as I pointed out the potential problems.

Before hanging up, I told him I would at least think about it. Later, while musing over our phone conversation, I wondered whether this was the answer to the question I had posed to the Lord about what I should do next.

Getting God's Direction for Decisions

When making decisions and seeking direction from the Lord, so often we expect the Holy Spirit to speak to us through an officially designated "spiritual" person such as a pastor or a priest. To be sure, He does speak to us in this way, but time and time again I have found that God more often uses either the instruments most available to Him—ordinary people—to get the message across, or the still small voice of His spirit to our spirit.

I could think of many times God had spoken to me through Hugh and others and wondered if now He was speaking through Marty. The key was discerning whose voice was speaking: God's, man's, or the enemy of our souls. We must do as the Bible says, "Test all things; hold fast to what is good" (I Thessalonians 5:21).

One of the ways I have found to be most effective when seeking to discern God's direction is to get quiet before Him—not necessarily physically quiet, although that helps—but rather, quiet to the emotional tugs and pulls of thoughts and desires which can drown out God's direction. The Holy Spirit's direction will bring peace, not strife or confusion to oneself or others, "For God is not the author of confusion, but of peace..." (I Corinthians 14:33).

When making a decision, it is important to analyze our options in light of God's Word and His character. Does the course we're charting violate scriptural principles? What, if any, are our underlying motives? Is our decision based on honesty and integrity, or self-promotion and greed? Sometimes this can be hard to initially discern and we need the Holy Spirit to bring clarity to the process. James 4:3 says, "You ask, and receive not, because you ask amiss, that you may consume it upon your lusts."

Another question we need to ask when making a decision is whether it will bring physical, emotional, or spiritual harm to others as in Matthew 18:7, where Jesus warns against bringing offense to another.

After applying this process to my own situation, the prospect of working on the Committee was daunting, but also appealing from a professional standpoint. I had to be sure I was not just considering working on the Committee to appease my own ego. Were my motives pure when placed next to the James 4:3 text? I had to admit "Capitol Hill staffer" had a nice ring to it. Nevertheless, the stakes were high. I had two young children to think about. I knew several women who seemed to be able to do it all, working full-time and being a mom. But I was now a single mother, and working at a job that would take up a significant amount of my time was not something to take lightly. I did not want to sacrifice what time I did have with them for anything other than God's perfect will. After much inside tussling, I decided to go to Hugh's office to see how I would react to being there, but mostly to think, pray, and hopefully get an answer.

It was hot in the Committee office. September was giving D.C. one last blast of Indian summer. The Committee's suite of offices was deserted. I supposed the powers that be were waiting for more time to pass before decisions would be made and life could move on. Feeling slightly overwhelmed, I leaned against the doorframe to Hugh's cubicle. The air seemed stale. *Hugh was probably the last one to set foot in here*, I thought to myself. Slowly, I scanned the room, taking in the muted gray overtones of his office, his desk, the walls, and the floor, deflected only in part by the eclectic disarray of his possessions. His bright red, white, and blue "I Love DC" coffee cup was perched precariously on the shelf overhanging his desk; stacks of papers were piled high in the "In" and "Out" boxes; a vivid green poster of the continent of Africa, overlaid by the cherubic faces of scores of African children, hung on the wall; and his suit jacket was draped casually over the back of his chair. This was almost the straw that broke the camel's back, causing me momentarily to wish I was somewhere else. I averted my gaze. *Had I made the wrong decision to come here?* I questioned, fighting to hold back the tears. *These were Hugh's things. This was Hugh's office. This was Hugh's jacket, the one we had picked out together.* My gaze returned to the chair and the dark blue jacket spread wide across its frame. Leaning over, I gathered the jacket in my hands, brought it up to my nose, and inhaled deeply. *Hugh.*

I opened one of his desk drawers and rumbled through the crumpled paper, staples, and pencils. I wanted to touch things that he had touched. With a deep sigh, I swiveled his chair around and plopped down. *I came here to make a decision,* I thought, trying to recapture my rapidly fading sense of determination. Looking up at the ceiling, I began to go over my options. I could play it safe and go back to the position with the City; have a set schedule with my children, which would be helpful at their young ages; or I could take a chance to work on the Committee with all of its unpredictability and public speaking. *Hmm, doesn't sound like much of a choice*, I thought to myself. But then again, the

Committee could also be a gateway into the international policy arena, a career choice that would impact me for years to come. "Hugh what should I do?" My voice quaked, pleading aloud for an answer from a voice I would never hear again. *Could I work in a place that reminded me of you every day?* I wasn't sure. *Could I do the work of a congressional staff person?* I was admittedly a little nervous about what the job might entail. Although I was a lawyer, I was not steeped in the legislative policy stuff that most people who worked here seemed to eat for breakfast. And the thought of public speaking made my palms sweat. Yet even as doubts pulled at my heart, I knew that if I passed up this opportunity, I was passing up more than a job. Deep down inside I knew that I would be passing up another chance to cross the threshold into what God had planned for my life by giving in to my doubts and fears.

I closed my eyes, relinquishing my gaze from a picture on the wall of Hugh smiling, his arms around several other staff members with Mickey Leland in the center. I prayed, *Lord, please help me. Tell me what to do. Give me the courage that I need to go on without Hugh.* Leaning back in Hugh's chair, my eyes closed tight, the tears that had begun to flow a few minutes before stopped, and the realization that all of this—Hugh's death, my being here—all of it was known and had been known by God. *What did Psalm 139 say?*

Your eyes saw my substance, being yet unformed. And in Your book they all were written. The days fashioned for me, when as yet there were none of them (Psalm 139:16).

As I mused about the future and the sense of calm that had suddenly permeated my thoughts, I felt confident about what I would do next. I finally had a sense of peace about the direction I should take. James 4:17 states, "Nor is God's wisdom of an earthly nature, but...is first pure, then peaceable, gentle and easy to be entreated, full of mercy and good fruits, without partiality, without hypocrisy." This peace was confirmation to me that the Lord was directing my steps. How strange it all seemed, knowing that I was going to apply for a job similar to Hugh's and perhaps even work in the same office. Instead of going backwards, however, I was moving forward, into another time and season of my life.

Four months later on a crisp and sunny January morning, I made my way toward the Rayburn House Office building for my first day on the job. A chilly winter's wind was blowing through the massive oak trees that flanked the street. I imagined it was the angels cheering me on as the sparsely laden branches were thrust forward by the breeze. I walked gingerly up the busy street, crowded during the morning rush hour with Capitol Hill police directing traffic, lobbyists making their way to important meetings, small crowds of staffers walking briskly alongside a Congressman or Congresswoman. *This was the world that I had come to*, I thought with a note of trepidation that caused my pace to slow.

Glancing across the street, I caught a glimpse of a beautiful ornate fountain, its flow silenced for the winter, a few forlorn leaves rustling around its base. *Hugh and I sat along the benches that lined that foun-*

tain just last spring to have lunch, I thought to myself. The great oaks were in bloom then, and water had splashed playfully from the flouted spout that stood majestically in its center.

Unbelievable that so much can happen in such a short time. I let out a long sigh, turned my gaze from the fountain, my thoughts a mixture of sadness and acceptance, and continued walking up the hill. *The first of many flashbacks,* I thought pensively.

No sooner had I reached the entrance to the building than flashback number two greeted me. The guard, who always had a smile on his face and knew me only as the woman with the two little babies who sometimes picked up her husband when he worked late, was standing at the guard's desk as I walked through the door. My heart beat a little faster as I saw a momentary look of surprise dart across his face. I wondered if he knew I was working here, and what that look meant. The knot in my stomach grew tighter. With an air of feigned confidence, I proceeded straight for the security gate, and smiling broadly I said, "Hi, how are you doing?"

He hesitated just a moment, and then responded with, "Doing well. How're those sweet babies?"

"They're coming along pretty well," I replied, wanting my purse to hurry through the x-ray machine. I didn't feel like giving any explanations. Quickly grabbing it as it came through the opening, I gave a swift glance back at him and said a bit too loudly, "You take care, okay?"

"You do the same ma'am. You do the same."

Chapter 4: Study Questions

1. How do you go about making major decisions?
2. How do you know when the Holy Spirit is leading you?
3. Are there any lingering areas of fear in your life that may impact your decision-making process?

1. Pros + Cons
   Pray about it

2. After praying about it, I examine how I am feeling about decision. Feel peace and contentment

3. Of late fear getting ill in foreign land

Chapter 5

Once You Hear, Take the Step

I can do everything through him who gives me strength (Philippians 4:13).

Walking into the offices of Congressman Tony P. Hall, you get the feeling he has an interesting story to tell, his life revealed in measure through a myriad of framed snapshots. Emaciated limbs and distended bellies were sandwiched between formal gowns and smiling presidents—a kaleidoscope of memories and history lined the walls.

For more than two decades, Congressman Hall had worked diligently on Capitol Hill, devoting most of his career towards the lofty goal of ending world hunger. I had met him while interviewing for my position on the Committee. In the short time I was with him, I had been impressed with the quiet intensity he seemed to possess about his cause. Congressman Hall had assumed the role of Committee Chair after Mickey Leland's death, and the contrast between the two was stark. Tony Hall was as understated as Mickey Leland had been flamboyant. Yet the photos spoke of a commonality between the two of them—a determination to use their places of authority as U.S. Congressmen to open the eyes and the pocketbooks of the world to the plight of those plagued by hunger and poverty.

Removing my gaze from the pictures, I quickly took in the outer office. A small lamp sat on top of the receptionist's desk and gave off a pleasant warm glow, muting the somewhat cavernous feeling one received while walking through the halls of the Rayburn building. Space appeared to be at a premium. Crammed into the outer office catty corner to the receptionist's desk was a brown leather sofa positioned behind a worn, but sturdy looking, wooden cocktail table strewn with magazines. Barely visible behind a hutch on his desk, the receptionist put the phone down and brusquely asked if he could help me.

"Yes," I replied. "I'm here for the staff meeting of the Hunger Committee."

"Oh," he said, more cordially, "Right in there," pointing me towards the door of the Congressman's inner office.

This room, in contrast to the outer office, had a feeling of spaciousness, with a large ornate wooden desk situated at the base of a huge window that framed the U.S. Capitol building, visible in the distance. The American flag and the state flag of Ohio, the Congressman's home state, flanked each side of the desk. A comfortable looking chintz sofa took up one wall, bordered by three matching chairs. Surrounding the sofa and chairs in a semi-circle were approximately ten standard regulation metal folding chairs. *Who sat where?* I wondered. I wanted to sit on one of the matching chairs, but my instincts told me there was probably a hierarchy of comfortable seat placement. After all, this was the Hill, and if I had learned anything from Hugh and my brief interaction over the last couple of months with people who worked in Congress, power was based on proximity to power, even if it was just sitting next to someone on a couch. I began making my way towards one of the metal folding chairs. My guess was that there were at least 15 people in the room, and although the room was large enough to contain everyone, it felt crowded.

This would be my first meeting with most of the staff, although I had met a couple of them briefly a month ago while I was gathering information on the Committee. I knew two staff members from the time when Hugh worked on the Committee, a time that now seemed like ages ago. *I hope the transition from co-worker of Hugh to co-worker of Patricia will go smoothly.* I had had some interesting lessons in the last few months on how people deal with death, especially the unexpected death of someone young. On more occasions than I could remember, I found myself bailing someone out of their uneasiness with me because they didn't know what to say. For me, the strain was walking around with this "everything's okay" attitude even when it wasn't, just because people couldn't handle anything weightier. I was beginning to accept the fact that most of us, just don't know how to deal with death. Accepting that apparent reality made it easier for me to accept the rise in tension I sensed whenever I encountered someone who knew my situation.

Armed with a smile and trying to look at least mildly confident, I made my way around the matching chairs, nodding at everyone within eye contact, and sat down on one of the metal chairs. Glancing at the morning agenda, I hoped I had done it all in one fluid motion.

Slowly, I began to exhale, letting out the air as imperceptibly as possible. Congressman Hall took a seat in one of the matching chairs so that everyone could see him. He introduced himself, asking us to call him Tony, and then introduced the staff director, who I noticed was seated right next to him in one of the other chairs. Looking around the semi-circle, I noticed Laura, one of the staff members who had worked with Hugh. I had gleaned from conversations with others that she was well respected on the Hill and throughout the hunger advocacy community for her expertise on domestic hunger issues. Catching my gaze, she winked and I nodded back, immediately feeling like I had a friend. Mike, who was sitting next to Laura, was another veteran of the Mickey days. While Laura was the expert on domestic hunger, Mike held that title when it came to international issues. He had called me a couple of times at home during the months before the Committee convened, offering words of comfort and any assistance in making the transition to the job. His kind words had immediately won him a place in my heart. Besides one other staff member on the Republican side of the Committee, Laura and Mike were also the only holdovers from Mickey's days as chairman. Their reassuring presence gave me a sense of connection to the past and to Hugh. It also, in some way, affirmed me in my present role as their new colleague.

Tony was asking us to go around the circle and tell our names, give a little background about ourselves, and tell what our hopes were for the Committee for the upcoming year. *Oh, please,* I panicked. *Why do they always have to do this? Everyone here is a grown up. Can't we be trusted to get to know one another on our own?* My throat began to constrict and my palms began to sweat. *What am I going to say?* My mind scrambled to remember every fact I'd ever heard or read about hunger. I quickly assessed how many people had to speak before me, calculating that I had at least a couple of minutes to gather my thoughts. *Thoughts, what thoughts,* I screamed inwardly. *I had no thoughts about hunger except that my stomach was grumbling because I hadn't eaten breakfast. Get yourself together Patricia. You're a thirty-one-year-old lawyer. Come on now, or they will know they made a huge mistake in hiring you. What was my reason again for taking this job?* Three more people until my turn, I realized with a surge of panic.

For as long as I could remember, public speaking had terrified me. Law school had done little to cure me of this fear; it just gave me more opportunities to be confronted with it. The only way I could ever face the prospect of speaking was to write down in advance what I planned to say. As long as I could prepare a written answer of some form, I had the security of knowing I had the words right in front of me in case my mind went blank. I had never liked this extemporaneous kind of talk I was being asked to do now.

But then I remembered the sense of peace I had experienced in Hugh's office while contemplating whether to apply for the job. *If He led me here, then He will give me what I need to succeed.*

His Presence Equips

For many of us, fear, insecurities and past experiences with failure will often rear their ugly heads when we're expanding our sphere of influence, either personally or professionally. We need to remember that it is God who expands our spheres of influence (Isaiah 54:2-3). To do so often means that He will call us out of our comfort zones. In His mercy, God doesn't leave us to our own devices to sink or swim in this expanded territory. At each step of the way, He gives us what we need through His presence and power operating in our lives (Hebrews 13:21). Psalm 84:7 tells us that we go from strength to strength. The Hebrew word used for strength in this verse is *chayil*. In addition to strength, it means might, power, or wealth. At each expanded level of influence, God enables us to successfully fulfill the commitments of the next by giving us the requisite power or resources needed. But how do we get this progressive release of strength and power? By progressively experiencing manifestations of *God's* power through His presence in our lives.

But we all with open face beholding as in a

glass the glory of the Lord, are changed into the same image from glory to glory, even as by the Spirit of God (II Corinthians 3:18).

As we progressively experience God's glory (the manifestation of all that He is), we are changed into a greater reflection of His image. We literally grow in our internal and external reflection of God, the personification of which is Christ (Colossians 1:15). In other words, His strength becomes our strength; His ability becomes our ability. It is as the verse says, "It is in Him that we live and move and have our being" (Acts 17:28).

Moses, A Past Example for Present Help

Moses was stricken with fear when God called upon him to become a leader to the Israelites and lead them out of Egypt, saying, "O Lord, I have never been eloquent, neither in the past nor since you spoke to your servant. I am slow of speech and tongue. Oh Lord, please send some one else to do it" (Ex. 4:10,13 NIV). God's answer to Moses was the same answer that He gives us today when we are faced with moving out of our comfort zones. God responded to Moses' fear by reassuring him that he would help him speak and teach him what to say (Exodus 4:12). Later, when the ante had been upped and God told Moses to leave Egypt to go in to the promised land, a journey that would involve fighting a host of formidable enemies, God again reassured Moses that He would help him. His help would come in the form of His presence. "The Lord replied,

'My Presence will go with you, and I will give you rest'" (Exodus 33:14).

What did Moses have when he walked with God's presence? He had everything God is, including God's wisdom to know what to say and when to say it. God's knowledge of the future enabled him to move forward with confidence, and God's supernatural power swayed both the Israelites when they doubted God's promise of deliverance and his enemies when they rose up to fight him. However, even with the assurance of God's presence, Moses was a man just as we are men and women today. He was subject to the frailties of the human condition just as we are today. Yet at the intersection of Moses' fear and God's presence, Moses chose to allow God's presence to lead the way, thereby receiving overcoming faith, access to supernatural power, and a relationship with God that precious few had ever experienced. "He made known his ways to Moses, his deeds to the people of Israel" (Psalm 103:7).

Sometimes, as with the case of Moses, the intersection seems wide between our abilities and God's provision. Sometimes the intersection appears small, but stretches us nevertheless, as in my situation where I had to choose to believe that God would equip me to do this job, including speaking at a staff meeting. No matter how wide or small the intersection, the result is still the same. Because His presence will equip us, we can experience peace and rest.

Okay, I had it in my mind who I was and where I came from, only one more person, I noted nervously. As all eyes turned towards me, I took a deep breath and began to speak. "No, it wasn't because my husband had been on the Committee as some of you might suspect," I heard myself saying. "I wanted to be a part of something that made a difference in people's lives...."

Again, I let the air out in measured breaths, not wanting to show how nervous I had been. *Finished,* I thought gratefully. *Hopefully, enough came across to show that I at least had a brain. Good, our time of group sharing was over,* I thought, noting that the last person had finished talking. *Thank you Lord, for your help—one more bridge crossed,* I said to myself silently, sucking in a short but deep breath of air. Kevin, the Committee's chief of staff, began to explain how they planned to reconfigure the offices. They were going to literally take down walls and reconstruct offices so as to bring a sense of uniqueness to the current Committee staff and lay to rest the trauma of the accident. That meant I wouldn't have to look at Hugh's desk everyday, a thought that brought sadness and hope at the same time.

Time Marches On

The days soon turned into months, and very soon a year had passed. I devoured everything I could get my hands on that related to hunger and poverty in America and in Africa—the two places my work was focused upon. I was feeling more comfortable with my position, and a rising passion for the causes we embraced as a Committee was growing within me. It didn't take much for me to get my dander up about the deaths of 40 million children a year who died needlessly from preventable diseases such as diarrhea and from the effects of unclean water. Public speaking was still an issue for me, but I had only been called upon to speak a few times, and each speech was comfortably fortified with copious notes. Gradually, the dew was drying behind my ears. The choice to work on the Committee was a good one, I concluded, not just because of the nature of the work, but also because it kept me busy and the busyness kept at bay the depression that always seemed crouched in the recesses of my mind.

Some of my colleagues questioned how I could work on the same Committee as Hugh had. *Doesn't the atmosphere depress you? Aren't you always thinking about him?* were some of their questions. The truth was, he was constantly in my thoughts, and some days were worse than others. A smell, a random glance at a book, a conversation, or just a fleeting thought could trigger an avalanche of emotions in me in an instant. But on the other hand, the intensely gratifying and thought provoking work of the Committee was a way for me to channel my grief and helped distract me from the void created by his absence, at least during the day. Unfortunately, this distraction did not carry over to the evenings when I felt Hugh's absence the most. The offices had been changed significantly; so much so that I had to struggle to remember what Hugh's office looked like before I came on staff. Not so at home, where his presence was still felt in every room, and on the faces of my children, and with every hug I needed that went unmet.

The hardest thing was getting used to him not being

on the other side of the bed at night. *Was I always going to feel this gaping hole inside?* I was trying hard to put on a good face for Stephen and Dara, and give them some sense of stability and family. But it didn't feel like family any more. It felt like a crucial part of the puzzle was missing and you knew that no matter how many other pieces you fit around it, the puzzle wouldn't be complete without the missing piece. A year and half had passed since Hugh's death, and not only was I missing Hugh, but I had to admit, I was missing the presence of a man in my life. I longed to be held again, I realized with more than a little trepidation. The numbness that had shielded me from emotional meltdown and had allowed me to function as a mother and a Hill staffer was beginning to wear off. The tears that had stopped soon after I took the job were now trying to make a gentle comeback, sometimes triggered by a look on my son's face that reminded me of Hugh, sometimes just the faint whiff of a scent that carried me to a place where we had been together. It didn't take much. Life was beginning to penetrate my senses again, life that I wasn't sure I wanted to feel.

What did these awakening feelings mean? I questioned. To open myself to the possibility that I was feeling lonely or emotionally and physically needy was to open myself up to the possibility that I might never have those needs met.

What, No Sex?

After much talking and a lot of praying during our

courtship, I had finally agreed with Hugh that it was best to wait to have sex until we were married. It had taken me a while to get on board with this idea, but eventually I came to embrace the concept.

One of the things I could agree with Hugh on from the beginning was that once the physical boundary is crossed in a relationship, very often you're thrown into a level of emotional intimacy that the relationship may not be ready to handle. "Keeping the clothes on," Hugh said to me one night, "forces people to communicate and develop a level of trust that will just make sex better, not worse, once they are married."

When I had asked him where this was in the Bible, Hugh directed me to Ephesians where it says that a man shall "Leave his father and mother, and shall be joined with his wife, and the two shall become one flesh. This is a great mystery…" (5:31-32). Gradually, I began to embrace the belief that there was a level of commitment that marriage required, which nurtured the true union of the mind, body, and spirit of the individuals, creating the oneness spoken of in the scripture. On a personal level, the day arrived when Hugh and I were married and embarked on a wonderful relationship spiritually, emotionally, and physically.

But now, staring at the image in the mirror, and at the empty bed beside me, I wondered how long it would be before I ever felt the love of a man again. Even harder to accept was the thought, *What if I never felt the physical love of a man again, because I am committed to waiting until after marriage?* I quickly stuffed the thought to the back of my mind, knowing that behind it was an avalanche of thoughts that would lead me to a place I didn't want to go.

How long God? Three years, five years? Beyond that, I didn't want to think about it. So I went to bed, staring at the empty pillow next to me, my mind drifting back to a time not that long ago.

Chapter 5: Study Questions

Have you ever faced a time when you knew the Holy Spirit was leading you to come out of your comfort zone? How did you know that He was leading you in this way? What did you do?

What areas in your life do you see evidence of the Holy Spirit's equipping process?

Is it realistic to think a Christian should wait to have sex before marriage? If so, why? If not, why not?

Chapter 6

Walking the Talk
Or Something Like That

There is a way that seems right to a man, but in the end, leads to death (Proverbs 14:12).

Eventually, commitment is tested. And so it should have been no surprise that my commitment to wait for sex until marriage would be tested. A friend from law school called to invite me to a party she was giving the following Saturday. Before hanging up the phone, she added that there was someone she wanted me to meet.

"Wait a minute, Gayle, what was that?"

"You heard me, Patricia. There's someone coming, and I want to you meet him. That's all, nothing else. Just meet him, okay? It's about time you got out and had some fun. It's been two years now. There's nothing wrong with just having a conversation is there?"

"No, Gayle. There's nothing wrong with having a conversation."

"What's he look like?" I asked, my curiosity getting the best of me.

"Oh, why should you care? It's only a conversation right?" Gayle playfully scolded me.

"Yes that's right, Gayle. But it would be nice if I had a little information. So come on, give it up, tell me something about him."

"Okay. He's nice looking, you'll like him. He's about your height and never been married. Is that enough?"

"Not really, but it doesn't matter. Like you said, it's only a conversation. What time do you want me to come over?"

"Eight is good, that'll give you two time to talk. I know you don't want to be out too late because of the children."

"You're a good friend Gayle."

"Thanks. See you Saturday."

Wow, I thought. *I was just thinking the other day about relationships. I wasn't expecting to meet someone so soon, nor was I sure if I really wanted to get into a relationship at this time.* At once, my mind flew into overtime imagining everything and anything. When I started questioning whether or not he should adopt my children, I had to put on the brakes. *Wait a minute, Patricia. Where did all of this come from?* The truth was, as needy as I felt, I wasn't sure if I was ready for a relationship. I still thought so much about Hugh. *Besides, I don't want to get into anything I can't handle emotionally or physically. Come on, Patricia. It's only a party. You can always leave if you feel uncomfortable,* I reassured myself.

It felt so odd being in a social situation again with so many single men and women and no Hugh. We had gone out occasionally after we were married, but since the babies came so quickly, our dates were limited to a movie squeezed in every now and then or a leisurely walk. I hadn't been in a crowd like this since law school, and here I was again with some of the same people. *Yuck,* I wanted to go home. Suddenly, I felt as if I hadn't progressed at all in the six years since I'd graduated. I'm sure they were all very nice people but there was something about being single again in a room with people I was single with six years ago. It took me back to memories I didn't want to resurrect.

As if reading my thoughts, Gayle suddenly appeared as if out of nowhere, quickly grabbed my arm, and steered me across the room away from the food and away from the door. "Come on Patricia, it's not that bad. Try to have fun. You should have seen your face. There's the guy I want to introduce you to. He's cute, don't you think?" Actually, he was kind of cute, at least from a distance. *Why wasn't he married?* My suspicions were aroused. Trying not to look as uncomfortable as I felt, I followed Gayle across the room to meet her friend. *Hmm, still cute,* I thought, as we drew nearer. As she introduced us, I started to slowly relax. His demeanor was low-key and even a little shy. His name was Brian, and Gayle's brief description on the phone didn't do him justice. He was taller than I—which meant a lot, since I am five ten—was of a medium-brown complexion, had chiseled features, and dark penetrating eyes. He had a great smile too. *Okay,* I thought. *This might be interesting.*

Gayle introduced us, telling him that I worked for the Hunger Committee. He nodded while she talked, looking at me with a level of interest that at once made me feel awkward and self- conscious. Suddenly Gayle found something she had to do on the other side of the room, and we were left standing there alone. He gestured towards a couch and we made our way to sit down.

To my surprise the conversation flowed easily. He was also funny, to my delight, telling me at one point to turn and look at Gayle who we observed staring at us with a smile as broad as Texas plastered across her face. His response was to stretch and feign boredom with a large loud yawn to which we all laughed knowingly.

After about 45 minutes of non-stop conversation Brian informed me that he had actually just come out of a long-term relationship and although he wasn't exactly jumping at the bit to get back into another so soon, that is unless the right woman came along...*Oh what is that supposed to mean. Am I supposed to jump at the prospect? He may be cute, but he's not that cute*, I thought indignantly. All of a sudden I was exhausted. I was reminded of the days before Hugh, when I had grown accustomed to my "make-believe coat of it'll get better," the days of Louis and not wanting to settle for less. I was so happy when I met Hugh, and I could put that coat in the trash. I didn't want to do this dating thing again. I smiled politely at a slight joke he made, rose to my feet and extended my hand. "Brian, it has been so nice meeting you. I'm sure we'll see each other again. But you know I have two small children and a babysitter that I don't want to keep up too late. So, I'm going to go now," I said, my tone flat and without the slightest trace of warmth.

"Wait a minute, Patricia. What did I say? Is something wrong? You seem a little upset."

"I'm not upset, Brian. I'm just a little tired," I said, deciding to forego a lengthy explanation. But in the next instant I had a change of heart and decided to be honest. *What did I have to lose? I was determined not to go back to those old coat days.*

"Actually, I was just sitting here thinking that I didn't want to enter the dating scene again. It depresses me. I know that I'm not married, but in a way I still feel married. Your comment that "maybe if you met the right woman" made me think you were trying to be some sort of player. So I thought it was best not to waste your time or mine and to just go on home."

"Well, I'm glad you were honest with me. I know what you mean about the dating scene. I don't like it either. I'm sorry about my comment. I really shouldn't have said it. Believe me, I'm not a 'player,' as you put it, far from it. I haven't dated since I began that relationship five years ago. It's true that after this last relationship, I'm not really sure what I want. But I do like talking to you and so if we could start over, maybe we could get to know each other—not so much in the form of dating—but, I don't know, just get to know one another?"

His penetrating eyes penetrated my resolve.

"Alright. I think that will be okay," I said haltingly.

We exchanged numbers and decided to get together the following week. I decided to leave anyway and signaled Gayle that I was going. She put her hand to her ear to let me know that she would be calling me. *Hopefully not tonight*, I thought. I didn't feel like talking about it tonight because I didn't know what I thought about it yet.

Brian walked me to my car and as I turned to get in he looked at me and said, "Don't think too much about all of this, Patricia. I've never been married and widowed, but I can imagine this must be hard for you. We're just getting to know each other. That's all."

"I know, Brian. I'm fine. See you next week."

Once I had driven away, I took a deep breath and all of a sudden felt like laughing and crying at the same time. *What was this all about? Where was it going?* My former hesitation was all but flying out of the window. *You know exactly where this is going,* I chided myself. *I am very attracted to Brian and I know he is to me.* I wasn't even sure if he was a Christian, which was important to me. Relationships were hard enough without having to deal with major disparities in values and spiritual beliefs. There was a reason Paul said in the Bible do not be unequally yoked. If you were serious about your faith, pairing up with someone, potentially for life, who did not share your values was only inviting conflict in to the relationship, if not now, then later. *But then again, I'm not thinking about marriage. I've only just met the man. Lighten up, Patricia. Yes, that's right I need to lighten up,* I thought to myself.

Brian called the next day as if to seal the deal we'd made the night before. We made plans to go to the movies the following Friday, which gave me time to get a babysitter. *Wow, he didn't even seem to be put off by the fact that I had children.* I liked that.

I put Dara and Stephen to bed early so they wouldn't wonder with whom Mommy was going out. I definitely wasn't ready for that kind of explaining. We had a great time at the movies and later at a late night restaurant. *It has been so long,* I thought with an inward sigh as I took in the way he sort of cocked his head to the side as he placed his order with the waitress.

Eventually I steered the conversation towards faith. Brian's take on the matter was that he probably didn't think as much about spiritual things as I did given what I'd told him about myself, but he did consider himself a Christian of sorts. He didn't like institutional religion and so he didn't go to church, but yes, he did pray occasionally. *At least he prayed,* I thought to myself. *Good grief, what is the problem Patricia?* I asked myself rhetorically. But I knew. There was a problem. I hadn't told him about my decision to wait for sex until marriage. It would be different if my faith hadn't been such an integral part of my life, but it was. Nevertheless, it had been so long. *Why don't you just see where this might go?* I thought to myself. *Maybe he'll start going to church with you.* But somewhere between the cock of his head and the strong arm he slipped through mine, my other arm had just slipped into that old friend—the coat of make believe. As the days progressed, I slipped the other arm in without a beat.

Brian was fun, attractive, and intelligent, and it had been too long since I had the pleasure of sharing my thoughts with a man in this way. I explained my beliefs to him about premarital sex, and just as I suspected, he didn't share them, but on the other hand he didn't pressure me to change either. "I'll just have to get used to the idea," he said. His words smacked eerily of words I had spoken to Hugh in a similar conversation, even though all the while I believed at least in the beginning, that time and my charms would change his mind. They didn't. I also realized I wasn't Hugh.

We went on that way for about three months, most of the time I did a spiritual, emotional, and physical juggling act. Whenever things got too physical, I pulled back. Whenever my mind told me to end the relationship because of my conflicts over the disparity in our spiritual outlooks, I put a lid on my thoughts. Whenever the Holy Spirit tugged at my heart to pray and to spend more time reading the Bible, I ignored Him. This topsy-turvy state of being dimmed the fervency of my prayers, increasingly making my words to Brian about the importance of my faith seem hollow.

We Do What We Want to Do

Why is it that Paul's words ring so true, "The things that I wish to do, I do not, while the things that I do not want to do, I do"(Romans 7:15)? The answer lies in our make up.

First Thessalonians 5:23 tells us that we are made up of three parts, the body, the soul and the spirit.

And the very God of peace sanctify you wholly, and I pray God your whole spirit and soul and

*body be preserved blameless unto the coming of
our Lord Jesus Christ.*

Using circles to illustrate the idea, the body is the
outer circle. It is the material vessel that houses the soul
and the spirit. The body is also the source of expression
for our senses. The soul, or *psuche* in Greek, is the
second circle. It is contained within the body and is
comprised of the mind, the will, and the emotions. We
see the soul and the spirit differentiated in Hebrews
4:12,

> *For the word of God is quick and powerful, and
> sharper than any two-edge sword, piercing even
> to the dividing asunder of soul and spirit, and
> of the joints and marrow, and is a discerner of
> the thoughts and intents of the heart.*

Finally, *pneuma*, Greek for spirit, primarily means
breath or wind. This word is used to describe the Holy
Spirit and the spirit of man. The spirit is the place in us
that has the capacity to perceive God and is housed in
the innermost circle. "But there is a spirit in man: and
the inspiration of the Almighty giveth them understanding" (Job 32:8).

The spirit of God communicates to our spirits, instructing us in His will and letting us know when we err
from His will. But because of our three-part makeup, the
Holy Spirit's instructions do not go directly to our
spirits. We perceive the instructions through our senses
(e.g., reading and hearing the Word), and then filter

them through our souls to our spirit. Unfortunately, the body may have become accustomed to conducting itself contrary to God's instructions, for example, engaging in sex prior to marriage which we are encouraged not to do in the verses, "For this is the will of God, even your sanctification, that you should abstain from fornication: That every one of you should know how to possess his vessel in sanctification and honor (I Thessalonians 4:3-4). Nevertheless, we do things contrary to His will anyway. Why? Because the body's actions have been rationalized by the soul. How?

The soul—the mind, will and emotions—has been infiltrated over time with:

- mindsets that justify our actions based on our past experiences
- a will that is set on doing what it wants to do, and
- emotions too vulnerable or damaged to risk change.

It is as Jesus said, "…the spirit indeed is willing, but the flesh is weak" (Matthew 26:41).

What then do we do? We strengthen the tie between our spirits and the Spirit of God by coming daily into His presence through prayer, worship, and meditating upon His Word. The results of this process will be a filtering down of the regenerative power of God's spirit to our spirit, penetrating and transforming the soul, and bringing the body into alignment with the will of God—a process revealed in Romans 12:2,

And be not conformed to this world: but be

transformed by the renewing of your mind, that
you may prove what is that good, and accept-
able and perfect will of God.

However, it all begins with a choice—our choice.
When He speaks, whether through His Word or with a
knowing deep down in our spirit, we must yield to His
voice, otherwise we end up stuffing our ears and hard-
ening our hearts and going our own way—a way the Bible
says can lead us ultimately to death (Psalm 95:7-8).

Amazing how decisions can seem so black and
white when they're only theoretical. But my how the
picture changes when reality comes into play, I thought
to myself as I contemplated my current situation. I remembered how adamant I was prior to dating Brian that
I wouldn't have sex outside of marriage. Now trying to
stick to my beliefs and dating Brian too was like trying
to pat my head and rub my stomach at the same time,
and I am not the coordinated type. Unfortunately, I
chose to do what I wanted to do and that was to stuff my
ears to that still small voice of the Holy Spirit. As a result, the voice of God grew dimmer and dimmer as the
pressure of my feelings increased. Tired of the confusion, and the sexual tension, one evening everything
changed.

The next day I called Brian and told him that I
needed to think about things, and I asked for his patience. He told me that he understood my feelings and
that I shouldn't worry about things. He wanted to make
sure that I was okay about what had happened the night
before and that we would remain friends. *He is very ac-*

commodating, I thought. I almost wished he wasn't so accommodating and would take a stand one way or another. His give or take attitude made me wonder again whether my initial assessment of him as a player had in fact been correct. He didn't pressure me, that's for sure, but neither did he make it easy for me. His amorous attentions were always ready and waiting just in case I wanted them. I couldn't blame Brian, though, for my actions. I went into this with my eyes open, and I, not Brian, decided to close them.

Over the next few weeks we continued to see one another although less frequently, and I began to ask the Lord for help in clarifying my feelings.

How Deep Did You Plant the Seeds?

While reading the Bible one evening, I lingered over Matthew 13, which outlined the parable of the sower. The verses seemed to speak directly to my situation with Brian. What I saw was that the seeds of my belief in waiting before marriage were planted in much the same way as the seeds of faith described in the parable. In the parable, some seeds fell by the wayside where birds came by and snatched them up; others fell on stony places where there was no earth and when the sun came up they were scorched; others fell among thorns and when the thorns sprang up, they choked the seeds; and still others fell on good ground where they brought forth a harvest.

My beliefs about waiting were planted in much the same way as the seeds planted among the thorns. The thorns in the parable were symbolic of the tugs and pulls of the cares of this world. When the desire for a relationship and emotional and physical fulfillment began to come to the surface, they choked out the beliefs in avoiding premarital sex that had been planted earlier. It wasn't that the desires for a relationship or physical intimacy were illegitimate desires. God had given me those desires, but they were to be expressed within the boundaries of marriage. Following God's way was hard to do because my belief in this principle of waiting did not have a strong enough root system.

In the parable, not only were some seeds choked by thorns, but some never developed an adequate root system. When the sun got too hot, the seeds just died. For me, my desire to wait was not adequately anchored by a strong enough relationship with Christ. In looking back, I realized my faith in Christ was relatively new when I met Hugh. Although it grew, it also took a back seat to my relationship with my husband. If I were to be honest, the roots of my decision to wait were anchored more so by my relationship with Hugh than because of my relationship with Christ. With Hugh gone, the roots of my decision were put to the test; and just as the seeds in the parable, the heat got just a bit too much for me to be able to withstand the pressure. In a nutshell, I was trying to obey the rules without the support of an in-depth and consistent relationship with the rule sustainer. That was the key!

I couldn't follow the principles in the Bible on my own, nor did God expect me to. Only through His strength that He supplied could I do as God asked in His

Word. God's strength was provided through His grace. "My grace is sufficient for you, my power is made perfect in your weakness" (II Corinthians 12:9). The grace is there. The strength is there. We have it, it's available to us at all times. However, we don't always sense its under-girding support because our relationship with its source is not as intimate or dynamic as it should be.

As much as I cared for Brian, I didn't want to marry him, and the fact was I did want to get married again. But if he wasn't the one, then I was wasting my time. Who knows, I might have even been missing opportunities with others that held more potential. Yes, I would miss Brian, but I couldn't continue with this ongoing, internal spiritual wrestling. God is a jealous God (Hebrews 12:29), and He just wasn't going to let me get away with all of this wishy washiness, as it says in James 1:8, "A double-minded man is unstable in all of his ways." I called Brian up the next day and told him that it was best that we stop seeing one another. Brian, true to form, was understanding. He hoped we could still be friends. I contemplated what it would mean to just be his friend. We would see. At least our parting was amiable, and for that I was grateful.

I was disappointed with myself for putting the make-believe coat on again, but at least I didn't wear it for as long as I had in the past. I attributed the brevity of this foray into the past to the increasing reality of the presence of God in my life.

It would be much easier, I thought, *if God would just take the desires away if I weren't going to be able to act on them. Lord, if you want me to be serious*

66

about this waiting thing, then you are really going to have to help me deal with it. I didn't want a situation in which, every few months or so, I just decided to forgo my beliefs and have sex, ask forgiveness, then stuff the desires until the next time. If this was really something God was asking of me or any other single person, then He must have a way for us to deal with it. Abiding, or maintaining an ongoing sense of God's presence, I believed was the key, but how to do this everyday, all the time, was another question.

Chapter 6: Study Questions

Are there any areas in your life where you consistently find that you do things contrary to what you know to be the will of God? Would you consider these areas strongholds in your life?

Have you ever sensed that the Holy Spirit was grieved by your actions or thoughts (Ephesians 4:30). If so, what did it feel like and what did you do about it?

Pray the following prayer over any strongholds the Holy Spirit has revealed to you during this time of self-examination.

Dear Lord,

I desire to follow You in every area of my life. I realize that I have been holding on to behaviors and thoughts that hinder me from walking in Your perfect will for my life, and from receiving the blessings that You desire to impart to me. Your Word says if I ask forgiveness from You that You will forgive me and cleanse

me from all unrighteousness. Right now I ask forgive-
ness for_____. Thank You that the blood of
Your Son, Jesus Christ has now cleansed and removed
these sins from my life. I ask for Your help to continue
to walk as You desire in holiness and in truth. I commit
my mind, my body, and my spirit to You anew.

In the name of Jesus, Amen.

Chapter 7

Staying Plugged
Into His Presence

*Now to each one the manifestation of the spirit
is given for the common good* (I Corinthians
12:7).

I f abiding is the key to a strong and vibrant connection between God's spirit and our spirit, what then
is the key to abiding? As little static as possible.

Quieted by my decision to end the relationship,
loneliness, single parenting, and the accumulating
strains of life rekindled my desire to pray. I found that
when life just seemed too overwhelming, I'd get down on
the floor in my bedroom and just cry out to God. I'd tell
Him about my disappointments of the day, question Him
about His plans for my life, sometimes get angry, sometimes wait in total silence. And very often what I found
was that the anguish, disappointment, or fear would re-
cede in the face of a calming sense of God's presence. It
was as Psalm 68:9 declares, "Thou, O God, didst send a

plentiful rain, whereby thou didst confirm thine inheritance when it was weary."

Problems, needs, and mounting pressures were a sure incentive for seeking the reassuring presence of God. With the mood on the Hill—cut, cut, cut—and rumors abounding that the Hunger Committee's days were numbered, I never knew what to expect from day to day. The sense of uncertainty increased dramatically when Tony Hall, defiant over the possibility that the Committee's funding could be fatally severed, went on a 23 day hunger strike.

What little energy I had left when I got home was consumed by the demands of parenthood. Between the situation at work and the crisis atmosphere at home, pressure was mounting from both within and without. Pressed for the quietly affirming still small voice of the Holy Spirit, I was definitely hungry for God's delivering presence, as it says in Psalm 107:9, "For he satisfies the longing soul, and fills the hungry soul with goodness."

Pressure may drive us to seek God, but once we've received His help, we need to learn how to remain in a consistent relationship with Him. Jesus used the word "abide" several times when instructing His followers about the linkage between a fulfilled life and a relationship with Him: "Abide in me and I in you. As the branch cannot bear fruit of itself, except it abide in the vine no more can you except you abide in me" (John 15:4). To abide is to dwell, to endure, to persevere, and to remain, according to the Greek definition of the word. Two things will help us experience the abiding presence of God: praise and repentance.

The Joyful Sound

Whether alone or in a group such as a church, there can be a palpable sense of God's presence when praising God, whether it is through song or with our words. Through praise, we focus on the things we believe God has done for us or for others. We can express our gratitude, either through the words of the songs or spontaneously from our heart. The more we express God's goodness or His faithfulness, for instance, the more the faith develops that God is indeed good and faithful. What might have begun with head knowledge soon becomes a heart response to a very present God.

Praise for acts attributed to God often trigger a deeper appreciation for who God is—with or without His acts on our behalf. At this point, praise and exaltation may turn to worship and reverence, and we may feel the need to even kneel or bow. We are in the light of His presence, "Blessed is the people that know the joyful sound: they shall walk, O Lord, in the light of your countenance" (Psalm 89:15). In this place of worship, it is just God and us. Yet, in this place of worship, the static can also show up.

Clearing Up the Static

Just as static can interfere with a radio connection, static in our lives—our attitudes and actions—can interfere with the abiding sense of the presence of God in our lives. The Song of Solomon talks about little foxes: "Take us the foxes, the little foxes, that spoil the vines for our vines have tender grapes"(2:15). The little foxes in this verse reflect seemingly insignificant sins that amass overtime and eventually wreak havoc in our lives. Little foxes can take many shapes and forms. Perhaps it is the small fib that so easily slips off our tongue or the outright lie entered on our tax return.

In my life the little foxes most apparent are the offenses that I seem to collect as so much spare change. Sometimes it is difficult for me to turn the other cheek when I think that I have been wronged. Instead, my pattern is to internalize the hurt, mull over the wrong, and stew in unforgiveness. I am learning to forgive more quickly, but an honest assessment often reveals several people are usually still on my list. Past conversations or things I have done may come to mind, revealing areas of pride or lingering bitterness. It is important to deal with revelations of where we fall short of God's will in our lives. If we don't, these little foxes—in plain language, our sins—can interfere, just like static electricity, with the divine connection to God's presence. The reason is that the unrighteousness of our actions cannot be comingled with the righteousness of God. There's a spiritual disconnect. Dealing with the sin in our lives keeps the spiritual connection strong and clear so that we can experience His presence fully and consistently.

Chapter 7: Study Questions

Why is it important to deal with sins in our lives that we may think are insignificant?

Are there patterns of sin in your life. If so, have you repented of these areas or sought spiritual help from a pastor or leader in your church?

Is there a difference between praise and worship? If so, what do you think it is? Can you see the difference in your times with the Lord?

Chapter 8

Is God Changing Direction?

Cast your bread upon the waters, for after many days, you will find it again (Ecclesiastes 11:1).

The message said, "Hi, this is Mark Lawson, calling from the White House about a position in the new Administration. Give me a call when you get this message." *Calling from the White House? Wow.*

The drumbeat to keep the Hunger Committee alive was eventually silenced with the stroke of a pen. The Committee's funding was gone and now everyone who worked there was gone too. It had hardly been a month since I'd made that unforgettable walk up to the White House gate and handed my resume to the guard in the little tower. At the time I felt I was casting my bread upon the waters, and who knew, maybe I'd get it, maybe not. The possibility of working in a President's administration was exciting, and so I prayed that if this was the open door to my next job—let it swing wide open! *Well*

Lord, I thought, *if this means the door is open, I am definitely going to walk through it.*

I quickly returned Mark Lawson's call and a few months later, after interviews and a background check for a top-secret security clearance, I was putting my belongings into my desk at the Agency for International Development (AID) as a political appointee. *My, my, my* I thought incredulously. *Lord, when you do it, you really do it.* As I put the last of my pens and pads in my office drawer, I marveled at God's sovereignty and His timing.

Fourteen years ago I had been sitting on a mountain cliff in Kenya gazing at neighboring Mount Kilimanjaro, contemplating my next move. I had just graduated from college and was participating in a summer long program to build a school in a rural Kenyan village. Gazing over the vast expanse of Kenyan plains, I hit upon the idea that I should try to work for the Agency for International Development. It was, after all, the U.S. government's chief bilateral funding source for developing countries, and I wanted to understand how best to help countries, such as Kenya, who were so rich in resources but poor in per capita income. Years later, here I was, not only working at AID, but working in the Africa Bureau to boot!

It was an exciting time at AID. Nelsen Mandela was the favorite for winning the presidency in South Africa. My job included working with my counterparts in South Africa on legal issues to ensure that the transition from apartheid to democracy went smoothly. I enjoyed the work.

75

However, the more knowledgeable I became about the processes necessary for governmental and social change, the more strongly I felt that the only way lasting change would come to a society was from the inside out. In other words, hearts had to change before laws were enforced. During my time on the Hunger Committee and now in the short time I'd been at AID, I had seen constitutions rewritten, wonderful laws inscribed on the books, and even millions of dollars poured into noble projects. But, if the political and social will to enforce the constitution and the laws, along with the desire to implement the changes that money could buy were absent, the efforts were only partially effective. For me, the answers were beyond the physical and psychological realm. The answers were also spiritual. *But how to do that at USAID?* I wondered. This train of thought was nurtured all the more by my increased participation in the work of my local church.

On Sundays I worked in the church nursery, and some evenings when the church was conducting a conference or special event, I came in to lend a hand stuffing envelopes or to do whatever other sundry job was necessary. Stephen and Dara were always with me and looked forward to these times because their friends from Sunday school were usually there as well. Although I enjoyed working at the church in my spare time, I wasn't under any illusion about what working in the ministry entailed. I had been privy more than I cared to of the behind the scenes frenzy to get the polished program everyone saw on Sunday off without a major hitch.

So much was involved in "ministry." Preaching and

teaching were just a small part of the overall assembly that made the thing work; the thing being an up close and personal sense of God's presence so strong at times that it could soak the grit off your week and heal scars compiled over a lifetime. It had been that wonderful sense of God's presence in church that melted my anger at God for Hugh's death and caused me to trust in His love again. But there was a cost attached to this sense of the personal presence of God on a corporate level in the church. The currency was in lives wholly committed to serving God.

I was committed and getting more so, but not to the point of going into the ministry. However, I had to admit the thought had crossed my mind. But up to this point it had only been a fleeting thought that I tucked down inside my mental file case for future rumination.

Is That You, God?

I had heard about things like this. I guess it's what some called a vision. I was driving on my way to work when suddenly, in my mind's eye, a scenario flashed before me. I continued driving because I could still see the road in front of me. I was in a church auditorium that looked similar to my church but not exactly. The seats were filled with people sitting there looking at me intently. I had a microphone in my hand and I was preaching boldly, confidently, and very enthusiastically. I had never seen myself like that in front of people, and I couldn't imagine that I'd ever be as bold and confident in front of so many people. I could be bold, confident, and passionate about the Lord in one-on-one situations, but I'd never been like that before a crowd and it was hard to imagine that I ever would be. The picture ended after a few seconds, and I continued driving without missing a beat, reflecting on what I'd just seen. *Was that really a vision? And if so, what was its purpose? Was I going to preach like that?* I pondered these thoughts until I got home and tucked them away again. Maybe it was my imagination.

A few weeks later in a phone conversation with Barbara, a friend of mine from church, I casually asked, "Could you see me as a minister. You know, preaching?"

"Yes, I could," came her reply.

"You could?"

"Yes, Patricia. Why did you ask me that question?"

"I don't know I was just thinking about it." I was actually surprised at her answer. I thought she would say something like. A minister? I thought you were a lawyer? But she didn't.

"Why do you think you could see me as a minister?"

"Well, you have strong convictions about your faith, and you're a good communicator."

"When have you seen me communicate, at least to a crowd?"

"I saw you once in church when you were working with the children. One day you had a whole group of them sitting around you and they were hanging on every word. I think you were reading a Bible story or something."

"Barbara, that doesn't count. I'm talking about preaching, not reading a story. Anybody can do that.

Anyway, that's okay. I'm not seriously thinking about it. It was just a thought."

"Well, if you ever do think about it, I think you'd be good at it."

"Thanks, Barbara." With that, I changed the subject and tried to hide the disappointment in my voice. *She doesn't know what she's talking about*, I thought to myself. *Just being able to read a story and put two sentences together doesn't make you a preacher.* And my faith, although stronger than it had ever been, was not as strong as I thought it should be if God wanted me to go into the ministry.

After we got off the phone, I pondered our conversation. When I really thought about it, I knew I wasn't ready yet for the ministry, regardless of the vision, if that's what it was. Questions still lingered in my mind about Hugh's death that I'd yet to entirely resolve with God. *How could I counsel someone else about death when I still had questions myself? No, I wasn't preacher material. At least not yet*, I determined with an air of finality.

As the weeks and months passed, a gnawing sense of discontent with my position began to take hold. It wasn't that I didn't like the job, but rather, I was increasingly entertaining the possibility of leaving the job to allow for greater flexibility with my children and to do other things, even working in the church. Often, after putting Stephen and Dara to bed I'd go to my familiar spot on my bedroom floor to seek God for answers. *Had it only been six months ago when I marveled at God's grace in helping me to get this job? Was the grace now lifting?*

How could that be? I couldn't see God being in a process that resulted in me staying on a job for such a short time especially when I was convinced He was responsible for leading me to the job in the first place. I delved into the Word, hoping to get some answers.

Empowering Grace

The traditional definition of God's grace is "unmerited favor." However, grace implies more than just unmerited favor. It includes the notion that God will energize specific activities within our lives with His power and ability that will enable us to accomplish things that we could not do without it. That had certainly been the case when I applied for the job at the Agency for International Development. Although my professional and academic background had prepared me for the position, qualifications were usually just the beginning of the process. It then took a series of contacts, networking, and then some, to get your foot in the door, unless you had the right connection from the start. To be sure, I had given my resume to someone who worked in the Administration, but to my knowledge, she didn't hold an inordinate amount of influence, and I hadn't networked beyond giving her my resume. Nor had I worked for the presidential campaign. So, as far as I was concerned, God's grace was definitely flowing when the door opened for the position at AID.

On the flip side, the term the "grace is lifting"—a term I'd heard bantered about in church circles—implies just the opposite. God is no longer energizing your current efforts with His power and ability and the result is a lessening in the ease to accomplish the current task. Equally so, this seemed to be the case for me. The earlier excitement of the job had started to ebb, and it felt like more than the usual "getting used to a new job" syndrome that sometimes occurs after a while at a new position. I wondered perhaps if part of the reason for the ebb was the massive reorganization taking place. I had been given the option of moving to a larger Bureau or staying in my current location within the Africa Bureau. I opted for the larger Bureau because that was where most of the projects I was working on were being transferred. The move necessitated downsizing all operations in one Bureau and gearing up in another. *Was it just the onerous duties associated with preparation for the move that made me think about leaving?* No, it would take more than a reorganization to make me consider leaving a job. This was more of an internal restlessness.

Perhaps the growing sense of unease was because I hadn't been able to spend the kind of quality time I wanted to with my children. I'd only had those brief months with them after Hugh died before I was back in the saddle full-time at work and I'd been burning both ends of the candle ever since. Nannies and day-care providers had been a mainstay in our lives. I'd been blessed with people who seemed to genuinely love my children and they in turn loved them. For that I was truly grateful. But good help with the children wasn't the same thing as Mommy being there, and I deeply craved more time with them. *Maybe* I wondered wearily, *my inner wrestlings about the job were God's way of telling me it was time to make a change.* These were the stuff of my thoughts and prayers for the next couple of months until one day things came to a head.

The phone rang. It was Michele, the pastor's wife, calling to ask me to oversee the International Fair we held annually at the church. I was honored that she would ask me to do this and excited because I felt I was bringing my love for international cultures home to the church. Sure, I'd do it, I told her without hesitation. The conversation soon took a turn to more personal matters when she asked me how I was doing. Like an avalanche suddenly set in motion, I began to spill my heart about the confusion I'd been feeling about my job and even my thoughts about the ministry. She listened and prayed with me and then suggested that I set up a meeting to speak with her husband, the Senior Pastor of the church. She didn't want me doing anything rash, and since he had been through a similar situation when he left the corporate world to go into the ministry, she thought he might be a good person to talk to.

I did as she asked and the following week I was in his office. Sitting back in the oversized chair in his office I began to unfold the last few months. It was really a tremendous sense of relief to finally talk to someone about it, someone whom I thought might be able to put this all in the right perspective. *Why hadn't I done this before?* I wondered. The Bible instructs you to seek godly counsel when you're wrestling with making a major decision. *You know why, Patricia,* I silently admonished myself. *You hadn't wanted to take these thoughts seriously. What if God was leading you to con-*

sider the ministry? What if? So I chose to keep silent, not understanding it was the Holy Spirit who wouldn't let the matter drop.

Chapter 8: Study Questions

Have you ever experienced a time in your life when God's presence was very real to you? If so, what effect did that experience have on your life at the time?

Can you identify areas in your life where you sense the empowering flow of God's grace?

Have you experienced a time when you knew that God's grace was lifting in areas in your life? If so, how did you know and what was your response?

Chapter 9

Sometimes You Can't Escape It

I will lead the blind by ways they have not known, along unfamiliar paths I will guide them (Isaiah 42:16).

I had an enormous amount of respect for Harry Jackson. If it hadn't been for his kindness and patience with me when I came to him for advice, I wouldn't be at the church today. He didn't know me from Adam when I called his office after the crash of Hugh's airplane. Then I was desperately seeking answers to my questions about death, life, and the relation of God to them both. He had taken the time to offer his counsel, and his comforting and wise words were a lifeline to my battered soul. So it was not a coincidence that I'd been at Hope Christian Church after my brief wandering around from church to church.

What was fascinating about Harry was that he didn't fit the traditional pastor mold. He had an MBA from Harvard Business School and had been very successful in the corporate world prior to going into the ministry.

When God called him to leave that world and establish a church, it was a decision, he recounted publicly, that required much thought and prayer. But in the end when he knew it was God, he didn't hesitate and hasn't looked back since. *That's the kind of perspective I need,* I thought to myself as I settled down to talk about my job. *Not overly spiritualized, but not void of God's influence. A balanced approach.*

He had been listening to me for almost a half hour, occasionally peppering my monologue with a few strategic questions. Suddenly, he looked at me very evenly and said, "Patricia, I think you should take a year and attend Bible College. That is, if you are pretty sure that you were going to take some time off anyway, which is what I think you said."

"Yes, I'd pretty much concluded that I would just take some time and do some independent consulting so that I could have more time with my children." The night before I had pretty much decided upon this course of action. Perhaps consulting would allow me to keep my foot in the international development world, spend more time with my children, and learn more about God. Sounded like a plan to me.

"Well, that's where I differ with you. If you can afford it, then a year in Bible College will answer any questions about the ministry and will also give you the time and flexibility with your children. They are in the school here at the church, is that correct?"

"Yes, they are."

"Well, the Bible College is adjacent to the school and you'd have a lot of opportunities to see them during the day."

I sat there and stared at him. "You think I should go to Bible College?" I repeated incredulously.

"Yes, I think it would be good for you. You will grow enormously spiritually. But then again, I can't tell you that's exactly what you should do. In light of everything you've told me, it does seem as if that's where God is leading. But it is a major decision that only you can make."

My initial shock at his suggestion was gradually giving way to a barely perceptible sense of peace. *This is where you've been leading me all along, isn't it?* However, I was hesitant to fully accept what was quickly becoming clear—a major change in my life was about to take place. Major and quick.

The first trimester of the Bible College began in a month. I didn't know if I could do what I had to do in that short amount of time. On the other hand, this was probably the best time to do something like this at AID, given the reorganization. I had almost completed winding down my projects in the Africa Bureau. I had yet to be assigned the new projects and so I suspected the amount of confusion would be minimal. *Wow Lord,* I thought, *your timing is something, you do everything decently and in order as the Word says* (I Corinthians 14: 40).

Still, I had to think about this and, most of all, pray about it. *This was not just changing jobs.* This was changing careers, vocations, a life transition for goodness sake! *Slow down, Patricia*, I told myself. I took a deep breath. Pastor Harry and I went on to talk about the implications of my decision but I had pretty much

86

received what I needed from him. Now I needed to know deep down in my spirit that this was what the Lord was saying as well. I thanked Pastor Harry for his time and advice and left his office, but I didn't go home. I walked around to the rear of the building and went into the woods that abutted the property of the church. The foliage was extremely dense, so dense in fact that there was a noticeable dip in the temperature when I stepped out of the sunlight and under the lush canopy of trees.

Anytime Lord you want to speak, I'm here. I didn't expect an audible voice, but I did expect that the slight tinge of peace I sensed in the office would have settled all around me now, consuming all doubt and fear about such a decision. But that hadn't happened. Instead, the slight tinge of peace appeared to be evaporating.

I seem to keep having these chats with you, I said, remembering an earlier time while sitting in Hugh's office contemplating taking the Hunger Committee position. Silently, I went on. *You gave me the peace then Lord,* I told Him, my attention riveted by a colony of ants making its way across a stick near my feet. *Please do it again. Am I really thinking about leaving my job and going to Bible College?* This is serious stuff. A lot of people had invested in me at AID. I knew many people would not only be confused, but some would be angry. *How could you just give up a position like that?* many would want to know. I understood the sentiment, but all I could say was that if this was really something I was being called by God to do, then my perspective was that I really did not have a choice in the matter.

And then what about my bills? I had a mortgage to

pay every month. The monthly annuity income from Hugh would cover my basic expenses, I quickly calculated, but that was it. No extras. I would be giving up a pretty comfortable income and I didn't have a husband to rely on in case things didn't work out.

Ok, let's look on the positive side. What were the advantages? I asked myself. First, and primarily, I would be able to see my children during the day in a way I'd always longed for since they were very small. I would also receive great theological training, another desire that had been growing in recent years. The Bible College was operated by the church, but accredited by a very well respected theological seminary. Finally, it was only a year program. *Besides, I did have my legal training, so if I decided that I had made a big mistake, I could get a job somewhere* I rationalized.

"Lord, this all started with that vision didn't it?" I said aloud, looking up at the trees that formed a dense green tent twinkling with white dots of sunlight. The air had turned chilly and it was getting late. *Maybe I'll get some clarity later,* I thought to myself while rising to my feet. *Maybe this is a mistake,* I thought with a creeping sense of deflation as I made my way to my car.

The next day I went to work tired, feeling heavy and weighed down. *If this is really You, Lord, then why am I feeling this way? Your yoke is supposed to be easy and your burden light* (Matthew 11:30). This decision wasn't easy, and I wasn't feeling light. The peace I had felt briefly in Pastor Harry's office had faded rapidly with the hours.

I spent the next few days alone with my thoughts

and with God, keeping my interaction with people to a minimum. In the evening I asked the babysitter to stay and watch the children so I could pray undisturbed.

Pressing Into His Presence

Why did I necessarily think the decision would be an easy one? Because that's the way it seemed in books or when you heard other people talking about their experiences with God. If God said it, then that's it. No confusion, just peace, right? On its face, it didn't make sense to leave a good job for something that would drastically reduce my level of financial security, with an outcome of which I wasn't even sure. But from a spiritual perspective, when I looked at the increasing sense of unease on the job without being able to point to a particular source of that unease, the corresponding interest in the work of the ministry, my growing prayer life, and hunger for God, Pastor Harry's counsel, and finally the vision, all together, it seemed to point the way towards Bible College. The disparity between the natural versus the spiritual inclination was reflected so well I thought by the words of I Corinthians 2:14, which states, "But the natural man receives not the things of the Spirit of God: for they are foolishness to him; neither can he know them, because they are spiritually discerned."

Sometimes what God asks us to do doesn't make sense to our minds. But our spirits, illumined by the Holy Spirit, affirm that it is God who is leading. The previous verse says it this way: "Now we have received, not the spirit of the world, but the spirit of God: that we might know the things that are freely given to us of God" (I Corinthians. 2:13).

The Holy Spirit is housed in our natural bodies, which, as far as I could judge, were still subject to the influence of things natural, like financial security, power, and prestige to name a few. I had only been on the job a year. Would God lead me to leave a place so soon? *Yes, I guess it's happened before,* I thought, thinking about some of the biblical examples when the spirit of God had led a person one place only to lead them shortly thereafter to another one. Joseph was one that immediately came to mind as he was guided by God to protect the newborn infant Jesus.

They Listened and Obeyed

In a dream, the Lord instructed Joseph to go back to Israel since King Herod who had sought to kill Jesus was now dead. Joseph obeyed and pulled up stakes with Mary and Jesus and headed to Judea, a district in Israel. However, enroute he was warned again in a dream to bypass Judea and to go on to Galilee because Herod's son was in Judea. Ultimately, Joseph settled in Nazareth, a city in Galilee. Why did the Lord instruct Joseph to go to Judea only to turn around and tell him to go to Galilee? The obvious reason is that Herod's son was a continued threat to the infant Jesus in Judea, and there was not the same kind of threat in Galilee.

Less obvious is that the Holy Spirit leads us progressively. Perhaps the reason for this progressive revelation is, as many biblical commentators speculate, so that He can keep us close to Him and trusting Him. For without that level of dependency, we would no doubt forge ahead to our own peril. Thank goodness Joseph was a man that not only heard God but who obeyed Him.

Another biblical example of what sounded like a change in instruction is when Elijah went to the brook named Cherith. Elijah had just prophesied to King Ahab that a drought would soon commence in the land. To sustain Elijah during this time, the spirit of God told Elijah to go to the brook Cherith where he could drink the water and be fed by ravens. For a while Elijah was sustained in this way. Each morning and evening he ate bread and drank from the brook. But the scripture continues, "But after a while the brook dried up, for there was no rainfall anywhere in the land" (I Kings 17:1-7). I guess that was a hint to Elijah that it was time to move on. I wonder if Elijah had a moment of pause when the raven's drive-through—or should I say fly-through—closed down and the water stopped flowing? He knew God had sent him there. God wouldn't starve him, would He? No, He wouldn't and He didn't. God was faithful as He always is to provide the next set of instructions. For Elijah it was a widow in Zarephath (1Kings 17:8).

On a more personal note, I definitely believed that God had led me to the job, and although I wasn't experiencing drought in the physical sense, I was experiencing a different kind of drought. I lacked the drive and motivation to continue in this place. *Well, I guess this is where the rubber meets the road,* I thought to myself. *This is where my life must yield to the spirit if indeed I believe it is God's spirit calling me to make this change.*

And I did believe it was God. So, I had a choice. I could ignore the call and continue the path that I was on, which wouldn't be that bad would it God? Or I could yield my will, my life, and my job to His leading and leave AID. Funny thing, though; although it was indeed a huge choice to make, the inner turmoil had me just at the point where I was ready to leap out of AID's doors. I guess that's the purpose in lifting the grace, so to speak. If He's not in it, it's not only not worth doing; it can get down right uncomfortable.

He Helps Us Move
To Higher Levels of Faith

This crossroads required an even higher level of faith than the Hunger Committee decision. Now, after two weeks of mulling, praying, and crying, I finally had resigned myself to the conclusion that this was the step to take. I was also confident that my decision didn't come from Pastor Harry or anyone else, although I weighed his and others' opinions, including that of my family and a few close friends. *Nope, nobody to blame but me and God,* I thought with a note of finality. Although I hadn't experienced the kind of overwhelming peace that I had expected and still harbored hopes for, neither was I anxious. I had counted the cost every which way. It would be financially tight, but I could do it. I had enough light to take a step forward, but not enough to see the whole picture. I was grateful that I had at least some income to rely upon. I had heard of others whom God called to make similar kinds of decisions with no manner of support in place. Prayer paid for food. *God was gracious,* I thought. He knows our frame, and this was about as much faith as I could muster for now.

Two weeks after the meeting with Pastor Harry and two weeks before the trimester started, I typed my notice of resignation. As I surmised, the timing couldn't have been better. I was leaving no loose ends. To say my colleagues were shocked would be an understatement. I didn't really do too much explaining except to those I felt obligated to. No one really understood and I didn't expect them to; I barely did myself. My family was a little more accepting and although they didn't completely understand either, they supported my decision, knowing I wouldn't do anything that would endanger my children's welfare.

I was glad I was still at AID when Nelsen Mandela won the election. The invitation read that in a month he would be coming to the White House for a Rose Garden ceremony with the President, and my presence was requested at the ceremony. I needed to RSVP by September 10th. Even though I worked for the President, I had never met him personally. I had just finished drafting my resignation, putting down the effective date of my resignation as September 7th, when I received the invitation. *I would love to go to that ceremony. When would I ever get an opportunity to meet Nelsen Mandela and a U.S. President?* For a brief moment I toyed with the idea of changing the date of my resignation to September 12th or 13th so that I could attend. But even while the thought was forming, I knew it would be a violation of my integrity to change the date just to attend the ceremony. The Holy Spirit really seemed to have me on a short leash, so to speak by calling to my attention anything that even smacked of being slightly self-serving. *No, I would have to meet them some other time.* Glancing down at the exit paperwork from the personnel office, I noticed the date I started the job. September 7[th.] *Exactly one year to the day. That was really something.* I had no idea that the date I thought I had randomly picked to resign was the same day I had started the job. Coincidence or confirmation? I thought it also interesting that the biblical number for completion was seven.

Chapter 9: Study Questions

Are you where you believe God has placed you for this season of your life, professionally, and personally?

In looking at your life, can you see a pattern of God's direction? Have you ever veered from God's direction? How did you get back on course?

Have you ever had to sacrifice something that meant a lot to you in the short run in order to obtain something better in the long term? If so, what was the process you went through emotionally and spiritually to arrive at the place of sacrifice?

Chapter 10

When Tests Come Your Way

*For you O God tested us. You refined us like
silver* (Psalm 66:16).

Talk about confirmation. Sitting in the class with
the other Bible College students—some young,
some older—I was deeply encouraged by the
words of the visiting professor. He had just shared his
background prior to going into ministry. He had been a
clinical psychologist with a thriving practice when he
heard the Lord's call to go into ministry. Encouraging us
in our decisions to come to Bible College, he then made
the off the cuff remark: "So don't even stoop to work for
the President if God calls you to work for Him." *Did he
know that I had worked for the President?* I wondered
almost aloud. *No, I didn't think he had,* I summarily
concluded. Pastor Harry was out of town and I doubted
that he called in to talk about the students. I was encouraged.

The days and weeks passed quickly as I delved into
subjects like hermeneutics and exegesis. My mind was

like a sponge, making up for years of a lack of biblical knowledge. To top it off I got the chance to see my children almost every day in school. Stephen was now in the first grade and Dara in pre-kindergarten, so they still welcomed a visit from Mommy to read to the class. There were times when I felt I could have traded ten jobs for the occasional moments when I got a chance to watch them with their friends during recess or sit with them in the cafeteria.

I think the Lord often initially pours out His blessings in a big way to confirm His presence in our lives, knowing the time will come when the memory of His blessings will be all we have to sustain our faith during times of trials and testing. Such was the case about a month after I began school.

The first test was in the form of a notice that my monthly mortgage payment was going to increase by $500. *This was unbelievable!* I thought angrily as I read the bill. In my deliberations prior to going to school I had calculated my tight budget on the amount of my existing mortgage. There was no room to spare, not even $20. I had calculated every expense from the cost per month of little things like toilet paper to bigger items like the mortgage and utilities. I didn't see how I could make it without getting a loan, going back to work, or taking money out of my savings every month, which I didn't think was wise. *Well,* I thought with a sigh of resignation, *if I needed to go back to work then that's what I needed to do.* I was open to it, but I didn't think that's what God wanted right now. I believed He wanted me to devote my full-attention to this year. This was definitely some sort of test of my faith.

I'd learned at different times, through experience and study, that God will take us through tests, not because He needs to know what we will do—He's God and He knows the end from the beginning (Revelations 1:11)—but because we need to know what we will do. The tests give us an accurate assessment of ourselves and the level of our own faith in God. They also help to build our faith as we pass them, and it becomes evident that God was there all along, even when things seemed bleak.

A Case of Believing and Endurance

Joseph received a dream from God that he would be a ruler of Egypt. But almost immediately after the dream he was cast into slavery by his brothers and then spent the next thirteen years in prison. Some scholars note that Joseph's attitude upon receiving the dream might have encouraged his brothers' actions. He was at least socially insensitive, if not boastful, as some believe, when he proclaimed to his brothers who made no secret of their dislike for him of his dream, "We were out in a field binding sheaves, and my sheaf stood up, and your sheaves all gathered around it and bowed low before it!" (Genesis 37:6). Nevertheless, we know that God had indeed spoken through the dream. Joseph's name means to add. I wonder whether at any time during his thirteen years in prison Joseph thought the years were subtracting from the plans God had for him (Genesis 37-50). But when it was all said and done, not only did God fulfill the promise to Joseph when he became governor over Egypt, but he had become God's man in the process as revealed by the words of Pharaoh, "Can we find such a one as this is, a man in whom the Spirit of God is? (Genesis 41:38)

It's sometimes hard to accept, but trials are often the only way our character and faith will be developed. Peter encouraged us with these words about trials: "For the trial of your faith, being much more precious than of gold that perishes, though it be tried with fire, might be found unto praise and honor and glory at the appearing of Jesus Christ" (I Peter 1:7). On the other hand, some trials come about because of our own actions.

He Did It His Way

Samuel was supposed to meet King Saul in seven days, but Samuel was running late. King Saul was under siege and his men were fleeing. Under pressure from the circumstances, he decided that, rather than waiting for Samuel, he would take matters into his own hands. He usurped Samuel's role as priest and offered the burnt offering himself, a custom of the day before a crucial battle. Although it seems like a harmless act, it cost him his reign as king. When Samuel got there and found out what Saul had done, he informed him, "You have disobeyed the commandment of the Lord your God....but now your dynasty must end; for the Lord wants a man who will obey him" (I Samuel 13: 8-14). The kingdom was transferred to David, in whom God found a man after His own heart.

Remember the promise God spoke to your heart when you made the decision to go to Bible College? I thought. "But my God shall supply all your needs according to His riches in Glory" (Philippians 4:19). *Well, now you will see if you truly believed that promise or not.* I had a financial need and, with a bravado I didn't necessarily feel, declared, *If it is God's will for me to be here and continue in the way that I am going, then He will supply what I need to continue.*

A Supernatural Answer!

Over the next few days, I consistently brought this issue before the Lord every time I remembered in prayer—which was every time I prayed, and that was frequently. Meditating on Philippians 4:19 and other verses that spoke of God's provision, my faith began to grow. What happened a week later might appear coincidental to others, but to me it was a miraculous answer to prayer! I received another letter informing me that instead of raising my mortgage by $500, it would only be raised by $200, due to a miscalculation. The next day, I was informed by the principal of the church's school that it was the school's policy to reduce the tuition for children of Bible College students, given the work the Bible College students did for the school. The net result of these reductions was that my expenses were back to what I had originally anticipated. I was overjoyed and filled with awe at the way God had worked things out. The joy, however, was not to last long. Test number two was soon to make an appearance.

A couple of weeks later at a routine doctor's visit, I told the doctor about pain I had been experiencing in my hands and back. She ran some tests and a few days later informed me that I tested positive for rheumatoid arthritis. *My, my,* I thought, *this was really something.* I hadn't been in Bible College more than a month and I'd experienced more surprises than I had in the last year. Although the news about the arthritis made me nervous, it also said to me that I was probably on the right track if I was facing this much spiritual opposition. I took the arthritis issue to prayer, but unlike the other tests, this one apparently wasn't to have a quick turnaround.

When Mom died

Chapter 9: Study Questions

Have you ever experienced a test from God? If so, what was the purpose for it in your life?

How can you tell the difference between a test from God or harassment from the enemy of our souls?

Why does God need to test us?

To draw us closer to him.

Chapter 11

Release What's in Your Hand

Humble yourselves before the Lord and He will lift you up (James 4:10).

As the semester unfolded, each day offered a new opportunity for growth. One day the instructor said, "Pray about something you have been praying over for a long time but have not received an answer. Ask the Holy Spirit if there is anything that has been delaying the answer, and if so, if the source of the delay is something in you." *Okay, I thought. This was easy.* It didn't take me long to pull out my wrung out, worn down, all too familiar refrain, *"Why haven't you brought me a husband?"*

It had been six years since Hugh died. And just as I had done so many times in the past, I began to rehearse the reasons why I needed a husband, why the children needed a father, why if God didn't bring this man to me, there would be dire consequences to all of our emotional well beings. After all, didn't He know the impact of single parenthood on young black males? As my tears turned to sobs, I buried my face in my hands so as not to alert my fellow students of how upset I was about this particular unanswered prayer. And before I could get out the next sniffle, the words resounded somewhere in my consciousness, "You will have it." *Have what?* I asked silently. The tears stopped immediately. *You will have it,* the thought impressed itself again upon my mind. I got it quicker than I had gotten anything in recent memory. I will have a husband. I sat up, wiped my face, a slow grin creeping out of the corners of my mouth. I stood up and left the room, so overcome was I by my newfound revelation. *God loved me.* I beamed inside. *He was going to give me a husband.* Funny how we measure how much God loves us by what we receive.

Once home that evening, I went to my room to pray and thank God for what He'd said, assuring Him I could wait until He brought the man, just so long as He brought him. Literally, before the next thank you could escape my lips, a thought skirted through the back of my mind, "What you have freely received are you willing to give back to me?" I ignored the thought. *You just can't be happy can you? You always have to find the cloud in the silver lining,* I mentally chided myself. *Come on, be happy. Don't try to get deep and act like you don't deserve a husband. God promised you.* "What you have freely received, are you willing to give back to me?" The thought impressed itself again.

"What, are You kidding?" I said aloud. I knew God didn't play jokes like this, so perhaps I was just confused. But even as I tried to rationalize it away, I knew it was God. It was exactly like the Abraham and Isaac scenario, in Genesis 22:2, where God asked Abraham to sacrifice his only son. Only I was being asked to sacrifice my desire for a husband. Thus began a dialogue late into the night and into the next day between the Holy Spirit and me. You would have thought I had the ring on my finger and the wedding night planned, I so guarded my gift of a husband-to-be. But that was just how real the promise had seemed.

The next morning, after several hours of what could only be termed futile wrestling with God, I gave up. I knew I couldn't fight God and win. I didn't know why I had even tried. Drying my eyes I said aloud, "God, if you don't want me to have a husband or my children to have a father, okay. I don't understand it. I don't like it. But I know I must accept it. I really don't have a choice. Do I? You are God." *I guess I could go out there and try to find someone on my own like I've done in the past,* I thought to myself with resignation. But in the end that would only lead to disappointment and frustration, twin cousins that always seem to find me every time I've gone ahead and tried to make things happen on my own.

"I really do believe you know what's best for me and will bring me the best choice of a husband. I'm not that choosy," I said aloud again, still holding out hope for a different outcome.

But it looks like even that's not going to happen now, I thought. A creeping sense of dejection began to overtake me. *There'll be no choice. This is really something. Well, I guess You must have it all planned, and even though I can't see it or even conceive of being happy without a husband or father for my children, I choose to trust You. Just help me with this,* I cried. *I'm really scared to face the future without the possibility of not having anyone.*

Getting on my knees, alone in my living room, I opened my hands to give the only thing I could: my trust. *Yes, you can have it. I give back the promise You gave me for a husband.* And then I went to sleep, right there on the living room floor. The last 24 hours had taken its toll on me emotionally and physically.

If you think an overwhelming peace flooded my heart, think again. I was miserable, at least for the few days following what turned out to be a milestone in my spiritual development. What became increasingly clear as the days went by was the extent of the control that the desire for a husband had had upon me. It had been consuming me to unhealthy proportions. As much growth as I had experienced over the last couple of years, I couldn't unequivocally say that if I had been married or in a relationship that I would have been as devoted to my journey with God. In fact, the majority of my prayers were for a husband. In a nutshell, the desire for a husband had been an idol of my heart. *How long,* I wondered, *has the children's and my emotional and physical security hinged on whether or not I remarried? Probably ever since I was a little girl and started playing with Barbie and Ken dolls.*

The desire for a mate is a natural one, given by God. But my sense of completeness, my self-esteem, and my ultimate source of emotional and physical security should not solely rest upon the state of matrimony. Yes, marriage was a good thing, but the major weight of my emotional, physical, and spiritual fulfillment is one that should only be carried by God. As great a husband as Hugh was, there was still a place only God could fulfill in me and putting that responsibility on him or on any mate was unfair.

When Self Leads the Way

Thinking about it a little more, I could see that when our desires lead the way, our actions follow, which may or may not be in our best interest, especially depending on how needy we are at any given time. For me, the years of failed relationships and unfulfilled expectations had proven this true. I could also see that the only way I could recognize the hold the desire had on me was to be encouraged to let it go. By giving the promise back, God was showing me myself.

As I pondered my experiences over the years perhaps most significant were the lessons of learning to yield "self." Psychologists have written much on the ego and id. One of the definitions in the dictionary of "self" is, "one's own welfare or interests." Another definition is, "the individual consciousness of a being in relationship to its own self." I was in no way an expert. However, this journey had taught me one thing I was sure of, that as long as "self" establishes the boundaries and direction for fulfillment, God is, in a sense, limited in His ability to direct us beyond those boundaries. This is because He made us with a will of our own, and accordingly, will not impose His will, but rather entreats us through His love and His guidance to submit our will to His. If we believe that God created us, sustains and guides us, then only God knows the place where "self" will truly find fulfillment. As I looked back over my journey, I could see a pattern where God was gradually helping me to dethrone "self."

I had questioned whether I should give up the job in the Administration to go into the ministry. The extent to which "self" needed the affirmation of power and prestige to feel good about "self," was the extent to which I could not progress towards fulfilling my God-given destiny, the expression of which was outside the realm of the Administration position. Yes, it had been difficult making the decision to leave. I had finally arrived at a place of achievement, and although it was an appointment subject to the discretion and term of office of the President, it was still a job—and a desirable one at that. But looking back, how miserable I would have eventually become. There had been a season for that work at AID. If I had stayed beyond the season, then I would have missed doing the work I was created to do for this season.

Taking this a little further, the deeper the death to self, the greater the freedom of the individual to move beyond the limitations imposed by one's experience, which forms the construct of our desires and even needs. Depending on the nature of these life experiences, they can either hinder or promote God's intended purpose for our lives. Over the years I had battled long and hard to become free from the expectations of others regarding my measure of success. Truthfully, I had a long way to go. I couldn't deny that I still felt the need to pull out my professional credentials every now and then, especially when I felt insecure. And I also missed the social status that marriage accorded me. But I did feel freer and more confident than I could remember feeling in a long time, a state of mind I attributed to my attempt, however bumbling, to let the Holy Spirit lead every step and every turn. It was only when I got on my soapbox and let "self" take control that I began to have problems.

A Living and Active Word

Thinking back over the weeks prior to this encounter with the Lord, I realized that the Holy Spirit had really initiated this whole process of revelation. Hebrews 4:12 says, "For the word of God is living and active. Sharper than any double-edged sword, it penetrates even to dividing soul and spirit, joints and marrow; it judges the thoughts and attitudes of the heart." I had been meditating on Isaiah 30:21-23, which discusses idols of the heart or things that take precedence over God. In effect, the scriptures had divided what was soul—an all consuming desire for a husband—from what was spirit—the desire for a husband, grounded in peace and the recognition that God was in control.

The next few days lessened in their emotional intensity, and mulling over my newfound wisdom, I decided to test the waters. Silently, I inquired, *Did You mean it? Am I really not going to have a husband?*

My promises are yea and amen. I didn't take the promise back. I wanted you to give it back so you could see what was in your heart.

Okay, so then I will have the husband, right? I thought I heard a silent yes.

I realized I still had a little ways to go in this arena of sacrifice judging by how eagerly I grabbed back the promise.

In a strange way, although the desire for a husband was still there, the giving away of my expectation for marriage had freed me now to get on with the business of being me. And without this test, I realized with a start, I don't think I would have known that I could trust God completely. Life, of course, is filled with ups and downs and the days ahead would reveal whether this was just nice religious sounding talk or if it was real.

Chapter 11: Study Questions

Are there areas in your life where you have limited God in His ability to direct your steps? If so, in what way have you done so?

not really To what extent do the expectations of others influence how you feel about yourself and or influence choices you make professionally and personally?

Have you ever experienced an Abraham/ Isaac scenario in your life—offering to God something that really matters—or know of someone else who has? How did you or the other person respond?

Chapter 12

God's Silence Speaks Volumes

Wait for the Lord, be strong and take heart and wait for the Lord (Psalm 27:14).

Six months and counting. The days were passing quickly, and no job offer was in sight. I'm not sure what I expected, but what I wanted was an offer from Pastor Harry of a job in the ministry upon gradua- tion from Bible College. *After all,* I reasoned, *that was the purpose of this whole thing wasn't it? To go into the ministry?* My plan had been to take the year to study. Although I hadn't verbally articulated it to anyone, at the conclusion of the year, my underlying assumption had been that if the Lord had led me to leave my old job, then He would provide a new one in the ministry. I still had trouble envisioning myself as an itinerant preacher, even with the vision God had given me; however, I could see myself working with international missions. *That would be the perfect marriage of my professional back- ground with the work of the church.* Besides, the church wanted to expand its missions programs, what

109

better person to run things? I could see it as clearly as I could see anything. *It had to be God,* I thought confidently. But why was I the only person who seemed to see it?

Pastor Harry knew my background, but had said nothing. Not only did he say nothing about a missions program, he had said nothing about me going into the ministry period. To be fair, he had not promised a job to me at the end of the process. *Perhaps this was just to be an intense year of spiritual development,* I mused one day when I was particularly disheartened, *and I should begin looking again for a real job.*

Weeks passed. Graduation loomed closer. I was getting desperate. A few times I even pulled my resume out, just to remind myself that I was still employable. But although it gave me a temporary ego boost, it felt like an empty gesture, not computing with the spiritual DNA the Holy Spirit had implanted in me when I left AID. Upon leaving AID, some suggested I seek a temporary sabbatical in order to study. I considered it, but in the end came to the conclusion that to do so would only prolong the inevitable, and in the interim, tie up resources that could be used for someone else. Although I hadn't received a lighting bolt of confirmation about leaving AID at the time, I still knew deep in my heart that this change was transformational, and that I wasn't going back. I left not so much having burned bridges, but rather, having laid them to rest.

His Silence Is the Nail
And Waiting Is the Hammer

The silence was excruciating. There had been some light, some direction, enough to make it here. *What was the next step?* I didn't even sense a "wait on God," as we are exhorted to do in Psalm. 27:13. I heard nothing. But soon a funny thing happened. The longer the silence waged on, the more convinced I became that God was speaking. More to the point, there was the dawning realization that His silence was the nail and the waiting was the hammer that was driving me to trust Him on a deeper level. This was the direction!

A couple of more months passed, and the year was almost up. I still didn't know what I was going to do. I waited. I prayed. I even fasted. I then began to rest. He didn't lead me this far to leave me directionless now. And then, He spoke. The scriptures suddenly came alive with keys to my destiny. What I wanted most was confirmation that for this time and season full-time ministry was where He wanted me. The answer came in the form of Isaiah 61:4-6.

And they shall build the old wastes, they shall raise up the former desolations, they shall repair the waste cities, the desolations of many generations. And strangers shall stand and feed your flocks, and the sons of the alien shall be your plowmen and your vinedressers. But you shall be named the Priest of the Lord: men shall call you the Ministers of our God: you shall eat

111

*the riches of the Gentiles and in their glory you
shall boast.*

The words spoke to me of the spiritual and practical
applications of God's plans for my life and of forging a
coalition of prayer, which builds waste places in the
spirit, and my desire to provide practical assistance to
others, both at home and abroad. The confirmation that
I was called to the ministry resounded loudly with the
words "men shall call you the Ministers of our God."

When the Holy Spirit illuminates a scripture, words
that, in times past, might have had no particular impact
upon you suddenly stand out in such a way that you
know the Holy Spirit is speaking to you personally. And
so I knew that with this scripture He was telling me not
to worry, I was on the right track. I was where I be-
longed. Two weeks before graduation—God's timing
might not be our timing, but it's on time, as the old folks
say—Pastor Harry called me into his office.

"Patricia, I've been praying about your situation. At
this time the only position we have open at the church
is as a part-time administrative assistant for the church's
elementary school." The salary was about a third of
what I had made at AID. "Think about it for a day or two
and get back to me. I can't promise you when something
else will open up. It could be a while so you need to
know that."

"Okay," was all I said, and I left.

*Well, I guess that's the answer Lord. An administra-
tive assistant for the church elementary school. Hmm,
it's not what I had expected, but then what did I ex-*

pect? A position as a pastor? Not exactly, but an administrative assistant in a school? Well at least it was a job and it was a foot in the door. I'd been praying for an open door. I didn't specify what type of door, I thought to myself, a weak smile forming at the corners of my mouth.

While driving home my thoughts were mixed. I had to admit I didn't relish telling my family and friends— those who had watched this transition and were eager to see where I ended up—that I was going to be an administrative assistant in a school. It wasn't that I had a problem with working in a school exactly, *but how did this fit in with my background up until this point?* I wondered. *What would my family and friends think? Why does it matter what they think?* came the inner voice I had come to recognize as that of the Holy Spirit. *Why did you go to Bible College in the first place? Was it for a position or a title?*

No, I answered. *It was because I believed that was what You led me to do.*

Well, I've opened this door, and I'm still leading you. All of a sudden I was overwhelmed with not only the goodness of God and how He had answered my prayer by giving me this opportunity when He didn't have to, but I was also extremely sorry for my attitude. It was pure pride and nothing else. The next day I informed Pastor Harry that I would take the job.

Wants to teach us to trust him

Chapter 12: Study Questions

Why is God silent sometimes? Has He ever led you and then seemed to get quiet?

How do you cope when God is silent? Do you get anxious, lose faith, or become stronger in faith? *sometimes*

anxious, continue to pray and return to confidement

Think of times in your life when a passage from the bible all of a sudden came alive. Did you know it was the Holy Spirit speaking to you at the time? How did you know?

What other ways does the Holy Spirit speak to us besides illuminating the scriptures?

- Through other people
- inner voice.

God will never lead you where the grace of God cannot keep you

Train a child in the way he should go and when he is old he will not turn from it Prob. 22:6

114

Chapter 13

The Divine Connection: Sowing and Reaping

Each heart knows its own bitterness...(Proverbs 14:10).

Stephen and Dara were delighted that I was going to be working at their school. They had grown accustomed to me being there while in Bible College, and now, to them, it seemed like a natural progression. I would be out of my school and working at their school. I marveled at the multiple impacts of God's ways. He was using my administrative gifts to help the principal and the teachers in a practical way as an administrative assistant, and my prayer life was growing dramatically. It was as if I had two occupations—my day job at the school, and my evening job as a pray-er.

The Late Shift

It was 9 pm. The children were in bed. My spirit listened for the leading of God's voice. The more I gave of

115

myself to prayer, the deeper He took me in my understanding of what was required to increase the flow of His life and power in my life. Most often what was required was the willingness to keep my mind and spirit as clear as possible of negative attitudes that would impair me from hearing and responding to His voice. The slightest thing seemed to prick my conscience. Maybe I was angry with someone and just wanted to be angry because it felt good. I knew it was wrong, but I wasn't ready to forgive and forget. I felt I had a right to be angry. I could get by with this until the Holy Spirit had something to say to me. My anger was then a barrier around my heart that didn't allow God's love to pour through and towards the issue He wanted me to cover in prayer.

Sowing and Reaping:
The Good and the Bad

The extent to which I submitted myself to God's leading whether in prayer or in acts of obedience, determined the extent to which I experienced a progressive revelation of God's ways in my life and the lives of others. What was also clear was that this journey with the Lord had levels attached to it. I advanced to the next level of intimacy and depth of revelation as I submitted to the character shaping on the preceding level. If I uncovered bitterness in my heart and let it fester there, I was the one who seemed to be imprisoned by my unforgiving attitude, not the object of my wrath. Bitterness was not something to play with, as borne out in the scriptures. "Do not be deceived, God is not mocked; for whatever a man sows, this he will also reap" (Galatians 6:7). Therefore, if we sow bitterness by making a judgment against someone and holding it in our heart—whether the person was in the wrong or not—*we* will reap judgment by being judged by others. This is also born out by the Matthew 7:1-2 which states, "Do not judge lest you be judged yourselves. For in the way you judge, you will be judged; and by your standard of measure, it shall be measured to you." Many scholars note that this scripture does not necessarily mean that we will receive the exact amount of judgment we sow, but rather of a similar type or nature.

Sowing Into His Presence

Sowing and reaping also applies to the transforming power of God's presence in our lives. The more time we sow into His presence whether through prayer, praise, or study, the more we will reap the transforming nature of His presence. If we sow abundantly, we'll reap abundantly. And what are we reaping? What the scriptures call the fruit of the spirit. "But the fruit of the Spirit is love, joy, peace long suffering, gentleness, goodness and faith" (II Corinthians 9:6; Galatians 5:22).

As I sowed to the spirit through prayer, praise, meditating or reading the scriptures, many of the spaces in me that had been reserved for my hurts—my judgment and my way of looking at things—had to give way to God's perspectives on the matter. The more I allowed His perspective to reign in my heart, the more I found

117

that I didn't try to love as much as I was loving, I didn't try to have joy, but was often overcome with joy, and I didn't have to try to have faith, but was often filled with faith.

The more I prayed and saw evidence in myself of the transforming power of prayer, the more I enjoyed praying. God's presence through prayer was becoming more real than anything I had experienced prior to this point in my spiritual journey.

Perhaps the greatest benefit of this increased focus on prayer was the growing sense of intimacy and trust that was developing between the Holy Spirit and me. I was growing to know His voice and in some small ways to understand His ways. Yet I still struggled with staying in this place of confidence and power. While in prayer, it was easy to be bold and merciful. Prayer was a direct touch point to the personal presence of God. There was literally a manifestation of His power and authority that clothed me while in prayer. Although I knew God's presence was with me always, that accompanying personal sense of His presence was not always apparent when I wasn't in prayer. Most of the time, the memories fortified me to get through the tough times, but sometimes it wasn't enough.

Chapter 13: Study Questions

Have you ever been full of faith while praying, only to see your sense of faith evaporate later on?

What ways can you think of to help you keep the flames of faith shining brightly, in and out of prayer?

Remember
- How God has blessed you in the past
- Pray throughout day
- Chicken Soup stories
  inspirational stories

Chapter 14

Decrease and Let God Increase

If the spirit of the ruler rise up against thee, leave not thy place, for yielding pacifies great offenses (Ecclesiastes 10:4).

Staying in the Flow

Sitting behind the receptionist's desk is a perfect example of the difficulty at times of sustaining the carryover benefits to my character that flowed from the presence of God in prayer. The last time I remembered doing receptionist work was when I was a temp during a summer break in college. *Am I making progress or what?* I grumbled aloud to myself. I wasn't feeling very merciful, powerful, or loving. I was still grateful for the job at the church school, but I was also getting antsy. I wanted to do some things I felt were more in line with my talents and gifts. Answering the phone was fine, but I had a whole reservoir of talents that were just languishing, as far as I was concerned. I had heard that the church was thinking about having a missions program and it seemed perfect for me. *What was Pastor Harry waiting for?* Perhaps a little natural encouragement would help move matters along, I decided. So I arranged to meet with him one afternoon.

Once seated in his office I tentatively began, "Pastor Harry, I would like to talk to you about my job."

"Okay, what's on your mind?"

"Sometimes I feel as if I am in a box.

"What do you mean?"

"Well, sometimes I don't feel as my gifts are being effectively utilized. You know that I have a background in international development, right? Well, because of that background, I always believed that the Lord would use my experience to help the church in the area of international missions. I'd like to do some work in that area in addition to my work as an administrative assistant." I stopped and gave him a long look, to give him time to absorb what I was saying.

"Anything else, Patricia?"

"Well, yes, there is something else actually. The other thing I wanted you to know was that the Holy Spirit has been developing my prayer life in leaps and bounds. I'm not sure what I would do in that area, and I'm not talking about leading prayer meetings, at least not at this point, but I wanted to put this out there for your consideration in the future. But as far as international missions is concerned, would it help you if I gave you a copy of my resume?" Pastor Harry looked at me with that same leveled gaze that he had over a year ago when he told me he thought I should go to Bible College.

"Anything else?" he asked.

"No. That's it."

"Okay. Patricia, maybe God is leading you to do these things. I know you have a heart for international missions and I know your background, so no, you don't have to give me a copy of your resume. But I also know two things right now."

"I'm listening."

"One, the current need in the church is administrative. We are not in a place in the ministry to do a large missions program at this point, and what we are thinking about doing we already have the staff for it. In all honesty, there is really not anything for you to do in that area at this point. You may have gifts in this area, but the season for their use in this church is not right now. Second, if I put you into a more upfront position in the church such as leading prayer or some other more visible ministry, pride would destroy you."

"What did you say?"

"You heard me. Pride would destroy you. You are not ready to move out into these areas yet. I've watched you, and I've been praying for you. I believe the Holy Spirit is purifying your motives right now, working a deeper sense of humility into you so that when the time is right, which I do believe it will be one day, all of the credit will be God's and not yours, a position, a degree, or anything else. Remember the scripture that says, your times and seasons are in the hands of God (Acts 1:7)? Well, wait on His timing and all of these things will come, especially as you learn to submit yourself wholly to Him. That means your gifts, talents, and how they will be used."

"I understand what you are saying, Pastor Harry, and I agree with the fact that the Lord is working a deeper sense of humility into me, but I have to tell you, I don't believe I am so filled with pride that I would be destroyed by moving into another place of ministry. I can't believe you said that. I just want to do the thing God has put in my heart to do."

"Well, you've heard my thoughts on the matter, Patricia. Continue to pray and I will too, but right now I don't see anything changing."

"Well, at least I had a chance to tell you what's on my mind. Thank you for listening Pastor Harry."

I left the meeting with a feeling of profound disappointment. Not just because I wouldn't get a chance to work on a missions project right now, but because I couldn't believe Pastor Harry had said those things about pride. *What about his issues,* I thought angrily.

Since coming to work for the church, I had been rewarded on many occasions with confirmation of the anointing of God that was upon Pastor Harry's life as well as on the lives of the other church pastors. But being up close and personal in this way also had its drawbacks. On the other side of the rewards, was the surprise of disappointing personality flaws of these same leaders, including those of Pastor Harry, which right now appeared glaring.

Father, am I filled with pride? Do I want to move up in ministry to be seen by people? You were the one who led me to quit my job and come here. How could I be filled with pride and do that? Your Word says out of the mouth of two or three witnesses let every word be established (Matthew 18:17). *So if You are calling me to do missions work and other things, then it would be confirmed right? Especially by the person that you've put over me in leadership. Maybe he didn't hear correctly? Maybe his judgment is clouded by his false perceptions of me? If that's the case, why should I listen to him in the first place? What if he never agrees that I should do missions or pray for people, then what? Should I leave this church and go elsewhere?*

Such was the searching of my heart over the next several weeks as I continued to man the front desk and pray at night for some kind of breakthrough.

Skimming Off the Dross

Pastor Harry's words cut, and I bled, not blood, but anger and self-pity. *Who did he think he was?* I asked myself defiantly. *God?* After wallowing in anger, hurt, and even fearful about trusting his leadership, I gradually felt the clouds give way to the crisp, clear dawn of reality and began to ask myself a series of questions:

1) First, do you believe Pastor Harry hears from God? *Yes.*

2) Has the Lord told you to leave the church? *No.*

3) Has the Lord led you up until this point? *Yes.*

4) Since you've seen that your attitude needs fine tuning, are you willing to wait on God's timing to bring about your destiny in whatever sphere He desires? *Yes.*

5) Do you believe God is greater than any obstacles that Pastor Harry or anyone else might put in your way? *Yes.*

123

After settling these concerns in my heart, my initial anger began to ebb. Gradually I sensed a greater openness to look within. *Maybe there was some truth in what Pastor said*, I admitted to myself somewhat begrudgingly. And then like grease, which solidifies on top of liquid that has been heated and cooled, so too did my issues slowly begin to take shape on the surface of my mind. Sometimes you never know what's inside until something happens to trigger a response. I might never have known that pride was an issue with me if this whole situation had not occurred. Like stoking a fire with log after log, I'd kept my emotions hot with anger by feeding my hurt with thoughts such as: *I've paid my dues...I've sacrificed...Who did he think he was?*

When I began to think about what internal script had been running during this mess, situations came to mind that showed pride had been and perhaps still was an issue in me. For example there was the time when one of my former colleagues on the Hill came to the school to enroll his child, and I greeted him with my friendliest receptionist smile, all the while hoping he didn't recognize me. He did. But truthfully, who did I think I was? Jesus was God and yet lowered himself to become a man. Was I so special?

I remembered the prick I felt when some of my fellow Bible College students were tapped to become associate ministers at graduation and I hadn't. Deep down I knew I wasn't ready to be a minister, but that didn't matter, I wanted to be acknowledged nevertheless. It didn't matter at the time that the scriptures specifically warn against a novice being promoted in the ministry too soon lest he or she be taken over with pride (I Timothy 3:6). After awhile I had realized that going to Bible college didn't necessarily make you a seasoned minister. That took time, working in the vineyard so to speak, which developed character. *I guess there was a reason Pastor Harry was the Senior Pastor,* I mused, a half-smile forming on my lips. Not that he was perfect, but he could evidently see some things in me that I hadn't yet seen as being a problem.

But beyond these revelatory moments, I knew that I felt wronged by his words, and my reaction had been to be angry and hold his words against him, although he hadn't spoken with any malice. Yes, it was a hard thing to hear. And, true to form, I took it like I usually take any criticism: I had gotten mad and let my anger fester. Yet even more detrimental to me, I had allowed feelings of unforgiveness to get a foothold in my emotions, which had nothing to do with Pastor Harry, but everything to do with my relationship with God.

And When You Stand Praying...

Mark 11:24-25 speaks about unforgiveness, a state of mind that can either promote or hinder the receipt of answered prayer:

> *Therefore I say to you, what thing soever you desire, when you pray, believe that you receive them, and you shall have them. And when you stand praying, forgive, if you have anything against anyone, that your Father also which is in heaven may forgive you your trespasses.*

If I wanted something from the Lord, these verses told me that I needed to forgive anyone I had something against. If I didn't forgive, then it says God won't forgive me. Further study revealed that this does not mean, as some may interpret it, that God chooses not to forgive us, but God is holy and will not condone or bless sin. Unforgiveness is a sin and as a sin it must be repented of as every other sin. Therefore, the sin of unforgiveness must be removed, clearing the way for Him to act on our behalf both in forgiveness and in answered prayer.

This principle does not mean that legitimate concerns should not be addressed if the pastor, leader, or anyone else with whom we are in conflict is conducting him or herself in error. Our concerns might be valid, and if so, there are biblical processes for dealing with such situations. However the bottom line is that someone else's conduct should not be the reason that bitterness, strife, and unforgiveness are allowed to pollute our emotional health and stop up the channel of communication and blessing between ourselves and the benefits of God's presence in our lives.

With a sense of peace beginning to permeate my thoughts, I asked God to forgive the pride that He had revealed and my attitude against Pastor Harry. Surprisingly, as soon as the unforgiveness was dealt with, the space in my emotions, which was once filled with hurt and anger, filled with an overwhelming love and appreciation for Pastor Harry as a spiritual father and friend. It was rare, in fact, to have someone who would actually speak the truth in love as the scriptures exhort us to do, about issues that could cause me pain in the future. Most significantly, this process had once again strengthened my trust in my eternal Father.

Chapter 14: Study Questions

Have you ever been at odds with someone in authority over you? What was your reaction?

What does God say about authority and what the leader and followers attitude should be towards one another in a given situation?

Are there any areas of lingering bitterness or unforgiveness in your heart towards a leader in the church or someone in authority in your life? If so, what is God saying to you about that issue now?

Chapter 15

In God I Trust

A bruised reed he will not break, and a smoldering wick he will not snuff out (Isaiah 42:3).

"**P**atricia, I think it's time that you join the ministry team in the church. What are your thoughts about this?" I was a little taken aback by Pastor Harry's words, but not totally surprised. Over the last few months, I'd had an inkling of something like this in my spirit.

"Well, I say okay. I think it's a confirmation of what the Holy Spirit has been saying to me."

It had been three years since that conversation with Pastor Harry about pride. During those three years I continued to wrestle on and off with the level of my responsibilities, and more times than I'd like to admit, I slipped into a rut of self-pity. Eventually, though, I came to a true place of acceptance and stopped haggling God about it. It was then that things started to change. My duties started to expand, and I even started working with the church's international missions program. It encouraged me to no end to know that whatever God's plans are for your life, they will come to pass as you continue to maintain the right heart attitude and trust Him.

Faith That Prevails

One evening after a particularly long day at the church office, I picked up my children from school. Looking back in the rear view mirror I noticed that Stephen was wheezing. Watching his chest for a moment or two I concluded that it didn't seem that severe. He rated his wheezing as a two or three on a scale of ten when I questioned him. But just to be safe, I put him on the nebulizer when we got home which seemed to help. It was December and I knew to be on guard.

About an hour later I went in to his room to check on him and noticed immediately that his wheezing was a lot worse.

"Stephen how do you feel?" He couldn't answer. "Stephen!" I screamed.

I immediately decided to go to the hospital. His chest was caving in and his breathing coming in deep gasps. *How did his asthma get this bad so quickly?* I decided to go to Holy Cross Hospital, which was closer than Children's. It had started to rain. *Great,* I thought to myself. *Rain and cold was a combination he didn't need.* I packed him and Dara up and put them in the car. It seemed to take forever to get to the hospital. Once there, they took one look at him, put him in a wheel chair, and carted him off. No sooner had I filled out the paperwork than the doctor came out and told me they were going to admit him. I wasn't surprised. He had been admitted before for asthma, although it had been a few years ago. I hadn't seen him like this since that last time. *How did it get this bad so quickly?* I asked myself again, as a tight knot began to form in the pit of my stomach.

The doctor led me back to Stephen, whose face was obscured by a mask to administer medicine. His eyes wanted reassurance. "Everything is going to be alright Stephen. But you're going to have to stay the night." He nodded. He'd been here before. Dara had been quiet the whole time, which was unusual for her, but understandable given the circumstances. I called my parents to come and pick her up for me as I intended to stay with Stephen that night. No sooner had I put the phone down when the doctor came over to me and said that Stephen was not improving as they expected and in fact was getting worse.

They wanted to transfer him by ambulance to Children's Hospital, but "Don't worry," he said, "ninety percent of these cases turn out just fine." I stood there in shock. I couldn't believe what I was hearing. *My son had to go to Children's by ambulance? What was happening here?* I was trying with all of my might not to cry, as I didn't want to upset Dara. I knew this needed prayer and lots of it, so I made my way to the phone again, Dara in tow, and called Pastor Lillie, one of the pastors in the church. She told me she'd be there in 15 minutes.

As they prepared to take Stephen to Children's, I began to pray. *Lord, why was this happening? Could this have been prevented in some way?* Shortly my dad came and picked up Dara. He hugged me and told me everything was going to be okay. "Try to hang in there, Patricia. He'll get through this."

"Mommy why can't I stay with you and Stephen?" Dara asked.

"Because honey, they don't allow children to stay at the hospital if they aren't sick, but Mommy is going to stay overnight with Stephen. So you go with Granddad and Grandma and Mommy will call you tonight. Okay?"

"Okay," my daughter said reluctantly. "Tell Stephen bye for me."

"I will Dara. I love you."

My father turned and took Dara by the hand, trying to mask the fear from his face. But I could see it. It was the same look that was on my face.

Pastor Lillie came and we stood by Stephen as they took him down the elevator to the ambulance. They wouldn't let me ride with him, saying there wasn't enough room.

"Mrs. Johnson, I will be with him the whole time. Try not to worry," said the doctor, who was attending him at the hospital.

Pastor Lillie drove me to Children's behind the ambulance. I tried to pray, but my mind and my mouth were numb. Once we arrived at Children's, they quickly took him upstairs where they put a machine that I had never seen before over his face. It masked almost his entire face. The doctor who rode with him in the ambulance told me it was pumping oxygen into his lungs. He then turned to me and in a very matter of fact voice while steadily watching Stephen said, "Remember, I told you that 90% of these cases make it? Well, that means 10% do not. I want you to prepare yourself for that possibility." I almost fainted. I turned to Lillie. "What is he trying to say Lillie?" I asked, my voice breaking with emotion.

"Forget what he said, Patricia. Stephen is going to be fine."

Lillie led me to a chair where I could sit down and still keep an eye on Stephen.

"Lillie, this can't be happening. He was fine earlier today, and even this evening the asthma wasn't that bad. I don't know how it could have escalated to this degree."

"I know, Patricia, but now we've got to pray and leave the rest to the doctors."

I looked at Stephen and he looked as if he were asleep on the machine. Lillie asked me to go to the chapel downstairs with her and pray.

Once inside the chapel Lillie began to pray with everything that was in her, calling on God to deliver Stephen from this attack and heal him completely. I watched her and tried again to utter some words, but none came out with any ferocity. I was almost paralyzed with fear. All I could think was, *Lord, my husband has died, now I know You aren't going to let my son die too, right?* Lillie looked at me and then spoke to me in a way that was the equivalent of a slap in the face.

"Patricia, snap out of it. I know you are afraid, but Stephen doesn't need your fear right now. He needs your faith and your prayers. You have got to get yourself together and fight. You've prayed others through situations

like this, now do it for yourself. Come on now, pray!" I
looked at her blankly.

"I know Lillie. I'm trying but I am afraid. I can't help
it." I just want to go back upstairs and be with Stephen."
But I knew she was right. I needed to fight and not with
my face buried in my hands. This was as much a spiritual battle as a natural one. The Bible says the enemy
roams around like a roaring lion seeking whom he may
devour (I Peter 5:8). Lillie and I went back upstairs and I
waited with Stephen to monitor his progress. Lillie
stayed with me a few more hours and then left.

Watching Stephen struggle for every breath even as
the invasive machine pumped oxygen forcefully into his
slender and fragile body, I contemplated what was going
on. This had been so sudden. It also didn't escape me
that this asthma attack had come just a few weeks after
I'd been ordained. *Was this a backlash from the enemy
of our souls?* I wondered.

Bigger Levels, Bigger Devils?

Elijah had experienced this phenomenon after the
prophets of Baal were defeated at Mt. Carmel (I Kings
18-19). His faith had allowed the enemy to be literally
vanquished by the spirit of God as he challenged the
prophets of Baal over whose God was stronger—theirs or
his. Jehovah God prevailed. It was a tremendous victory.
But shortly thereafter, Jezebel, the king's wife was so in-
censed at what had taken place that she threatened to
kill him. Elijah went on the run and the scriptures relate
he got so depressed that he wanted to die. This was an

example of a spiritual backlash. The enemy got back at Elijah through Jezebel's threats and the depression and fear that ensued. But God restored Elijah's confidence and delivered him from the fear and depression. He even led him to do further supernatural exploits later. Stephen was sleeping again, and so I went downstairs to the chapel by myself, Bible in hand to try again. This time, however, my attitude was a little different.

Lord, I know the promises of the Bible about healing. Because of the stripes of Jesus at His death and resurrection we are healed of disease (I Peter 2:24). That's all well and good. But right now I need to really hear from You. I need to know beyond a shadow of a doubt that Stephen is going to be okay and then I will have something to anchor my faith on. I'm not strong enough just to repeat these scriptures and believe. What I needed right then from God was His *rhema* word—a direct communication to me from God about the outcome of this situation.

His Presence Revealed In His Word

A *rhema* word is God's word to man. This is the same word used in Romans 10:17, "So then faith comes by hearing and hearing by the word of God." Hearing the word of God in this case is not via an audible word, *per se,* but rather the spirit of God communicating to the spirit of man through God's word in a way that evokes faith. The *rhema* word I needed from God was God's assurance from His spirit to mine that everything was going to be okay. I had read the promises of God in the

Bible concerning healing and as much as I repeated them, prayed them, and read them, the bedrock faith I felt I needed now was not coming. *I need a promise to anchor myself on right now, Lord,* I cried softly as I knelt on the cold floor of the little chapel at Children's.

Looking around at the banners on the walls, I wondered about the stories of the people who'd been here before me. *What was wrong with the children whose family members came here for comfort and consolation? Had any died? Had their prayers been answered?*

Slowly I began to turn the pages of my Bible, turning to the psalms with the hope of gleaning a word or two of encouragement from King David's travails and victories. My eyes lighted on Psalm 21:4 and I immediately pulled up and focused. "He asked life of you and you gave it to him, even length of days forever and ever." *Oh Lord, is this You?* I asked in a silent prayer. And then I knew it was. "For they intended evil against you, they imagined a mischievous scheme, which they are unable to perform." *God, thank you.* I began to cry and laugh at the same time. This was my *rhema* word! How did I know? I just knew. In my spirit, I knew. That's how *rhema* words work. God's spirit witnesses to your spirit that He's speaking and He's communicating. It's a knowing, and I knew. I stood up and began to walk around the room repeating the words and the remainder of the psalm, back to God. I then began to sing songs of victory and rejoicing that I'd learned in church and some that I made up on the spot. *Oh God, Stephen is going to be okay. Now I can pray without a doubt and be assured of the outcome.* I stayed about ten more minutes to bask in my reinvigorated state of faith and then went back upstairs to see Stephen. Half expecting him to at least be sitting up, I was a little disappointed to see that he was the same as I had left him.

Four days passed and he was still in intensive care and on that oxygen machine. His numbers hadn't improved much, and now the doctor was telling me they were thinking about putting him on a ventilator. I don't know why, but I had an almost visceral reaction to that possibility. Rational or not, I believed that if he was put on the ventilator he would not be coming off of it. No, I pleaded with the doctors, let's wait awhile.

Another day passed and still no change. Fortunately, my time spent in prayer on behalf of others had taught me that although one may receive an assurance in your spirit that the prayer has been answered, as was the case with the *rhema* word I had received for Stephen's healing, sometimes it takes time for the outworking of the answer to come forth into the natural realm. But it was less than two weeks before Christmas and I couldn't imagine being here for Christmas. *Lord, please show Your power on Stephen's behalf quickly,* I prayed again with renewed vigor.

I admired the doctors and nurses who worked in this pediatric intensive care unit. They were a special breed of people, I thought, to be able to do their jobs in this environment of sickness and sadness and still keep smiles on their faces. The parents of the little boy on Stephen's right who appeared to be about five or six had been holding an hourly vigil at the child's bedside. I had only been able to speak to the mother briefly and she hadn't told me what was wrong with her son. But I'd gleaned from overheard conversations that the boy had been here for a few weeks. I didn't know his prognosis, but judging from the low whispers and silent tears that fell from the eyes of relatives that came and went, it didn't look good.

The same was true of the little four-year old boy who was on Stephen's left. He was in a coma and had been in one for months. I overheard a doctor one day talking to another about taking him off of the ventilator. The look on the faces of the boy's parents was hollow and tired, but not ready to concede defeat. *Don't die, little boy,* I whispered one day as I looked over at the child who seemed a fraction of the size of what a child his age should be. You could barely see him down in the covers from my vantage point, *but Lord, as long as there is still life in that boy, please have mercy on him and his parents and bring him to full recovery.* With that, I stood up and went over to the child's bed and began to pray. When I finished, I went back to Stephen and looking down at the masked face, thought, *Father, we have got to get out of this place.* The intensity of the sickness all around threatened to choke out the light of hope that still flickered in me from my time of prayer.

The doctors came in again and said that if he didn't start improving markedly, they were going to put him on the ventilator. *God I can't fight anymore. I'm so tired. You said Stephen would be okay, in fact to quote You: "He asked life of you and you gave it to him, even length of days forever and ever." Remember? "Even though they intended an evil scheme against him, and imagined a mischievous deed, they will not be able to perform it."* Those were your words to me. I believed them. I still do. *Right now the doctors want to put him on a ventilator. I don't know if that's right or wrong. What I'm asking is that Your strategy prevail. Whatever You want the doctors to do, please guide them and let their own wisdom not prevail if it's not in accordance with Yours.* With that last prayer I turned to go the waiting room to try to catch a few minutes of sleep. There was nothing else I could do and either He was God or He wasn't. I chose to believe He was.

At about three a.m. a nurse came into the waiting room and began to shake my arm.

"Mrs. Johnson, wake up. Mrs. Johnson, wake up. Please come to the room."

"What is it?" I asked, my heart beginning to race. "Is Stephen okay? What is it?"

Before she could barely answer I was down the hall and beside Stephen's bed. He was still asleep as far as I could tell. The nurse then began to tell me the news.

"Shortly after you went back to the waiting room, the attending physician was checking Stephen and thinking about putting him on the ventilator. But then he decided to try something they'd never tried at Children's before. He had read about its use elsewhere on occasion. He injected Stephen with mega doses of magnesium. Magnesium relaxes the muscles. A few hours later, Stephen's lungs began to improve and his oxygen levels increased. This is the first breakthrough he's had since he's been here. If he keeps improving like this, I don't think they will have to put him on the ventilator."

I looked at the machine that showed Stephen's oxygen levels, and at the numbers I'd become intimately acquainted with over the last few days and began to cry. I sat down next to Stephen's bed and gently took his little ten-year-old boy fingers in my hands. *You answered my prayers, Lord, didn't You? You gave the doctor Your strategy. Magnesium? Wow, that was new to me.* I suddenly got a renewed interest in alternative medicine. *Thank goodness the doctor was open to hear You and try something different.* I hoped I would get an opportunity to thank him personally. I stayed there the rest of the night, holding Stephen's hand, being able to relax a little for the first time since this ordeal had begun.

The next morning brought a mixture of blessing and sadness. Stephen's numbers were continuing to go up. The doctor who attended him that night came by before his shift was over to check on him.

"Doctor, are you the one who thought about the magnesium?"

"Yes I am," he replied, his voice a study of detachment.

"Well, I just wanted to thank you for trying something different on Stephen. It obviously worked."

"Yes, I'm really pleased to see how he's responding. It's not a new treatment, but we haven't used it here at the hospital. I thought it was worth a shot since he hadn't been responding to the other medicines. If he stays like this, then I don't think we'll have to use the ventilator."

"I'm so glad. Thank you again. I really appreciate all of your work."

"No problem." With that he left. My words seemed woefully inadequate to my ears. I more than appreciated what he'd done. He could have brushed off that thought about magnesium and continued with the hospital's traditional course of action, but he hadn't. I would be eternally grateful. But my own happiness was overshadowed by what was going on behind the curtains next to Stephen.

The mother of the little boy on the right was sobbing and crying and the father was too. I didn't want to think the unthinkable, but I knew what had happened. A short while ago I'd heard a commotion at the bed and the nurses and doctors frantically working on the child. I left the room to give them space and privacy to do what they needed to do. I came back about an hour later. Stephen was awake and looking at me and looking at the bed next to him. The boy's parents were there crying and all of the doctors were gone. The boy had died. *Why did that child have to die?* I silently said a prayer for the parents and the family. I nodded at Stephen that I understood what had happened and sat down next to him.

He could talk a little and told me he was thirsty. "I'll ask the nurse if you can have some water," I replied.

"How do you feel, Stephen?" It was the first time he'd had the mask off of his face so that he could talk unrestricted.

"Better. Mom, that boy died."

"I know."

We talked a little bit more about it, but I didn't want to tax him any more than necessary, so I let the subject go.

"Mom, I want to go home. It's almost Christmas, isn't it? Will I be here for Christmas?"

"I don't know, Stephen. I hope not. Christmas is a week away so we'll see."

Another doctor came in and told me that they would probably be moving him upstairs to the other ward tomorrow if he continued to improve this way. They wouldn't give him anything to drink just yet as he had just come off the machine, and his lungs were still very congested. But Cheryl, the nurse who'd by now become my friend, promised Stephen that as soon as he could swallow and keep something down she'd bring him a big breakfast of his favorite foods.

"Waffles!" Stephen croaked out loudly. "I want waffles." It was hard to believe, but he hadn't eaten anything for six days; they had fed him intravenously. I bet he was hungry. On December 23rd Stephen left Children's and went home for Christmas.

Chapter 15: Study Questions

Why do you think God allows us to sometimes get to our wits end?

What does the bible say about healing today? (First Peter 2:24, First Corinthians 12:28)

Have you ever experienced backlash from the enemy of our souls? If so, what steps would you take now to guard against it?

Chapter 16

Miracles Do Happen

They will soar on wings like eagles, they will run and not grow weary, they will walk and not grow faint (Isaiah 40:31)

The faces peered back at me, and I was not afraid. The vision, I realized with a start, was speaking, "For the vision is yet for an appointed time, but at the end it shall speak and not lie: though it tarry, wait for it, because it will surely come, it will not tarry" (Habakkuk 2:3).

They're looking at that woman. The woman in the vision. I'm that woman, I thought to myself with a tinge of awe.

Eventually I moved from the school staff to join the ministry team at the church. It was a time of accelerated emotional and spiritual growth and joyously a time of supernatural healing. On a whim during a routine doctor's visit I asked the doctor to retest my blood for rheumatoid arthritis. A few days later the doctor called back with the results. Healed. No trace of rheumatoid

arthritis in my blood. Several years after that initial di-
agnosis of rheumatoid arthritis while in Bible College, I
finally had the answer I was waiting for: I am healed!

As I reflect back on the 15 years since Hugh's death,
little could I have foreseen the winding and seemingly il-
logical turns that my life would take. With the sharp perspective of hindsight, however, I can see the guiding
hand of God was always there with me, pointing the
way.

My children, now 16 and 14, are navigating their
teen years. At 6' 3" and 5' 9" respectively, Hugh would be
quite proud of them since they reflect many of his good
characteristics. But even more important to him would
be the fact that the words of faith that he spoke to me
many years ago are echoing in the lives of his children
today as they too affirm the blessings of physical, emotional, and spiritual wholeness that comes through faith
in Christ.

For me, the words, "We go from glory to glory and
from strength to strength" (2 Corinthians 3:18; Psalm
84:7) have become my banner cry.

It's sometimes hard to imagine that the same
woman, who was afraid to speak up in a simple meeting,
has overcome her fear of speaking so that she can now
preach and teach in other nations; or that this same
woman is now the founder of Life Change International,
a ministry of healing to the spirit, soul, and body.
Perhaps most surprising is that the woman, who couldn't
imagine a life without the man she loved, has learned to
be content wherever God has placed her.

Jeremiah 29:11 says, "For I know the plans I have

for you, plans to prosper you, not to harm you, to give you a hope and a future." Throughout this book you've seen that things didn't always look prosperous in my life, harm did seemingly come, and the dark clouds of depression, at times, stole my sense of hope. But there was also a pattern of my repeatedly coming to a divine intersection. The intersection may have been a place of sickness, fear, wrong choices, or simply not believing in myself. Wherever I was and wherever you are, meeting us at our place of need is His presence. Life can be very difficult at times, and the sweet sounding promises of the Scriptures can appear hollow.

Perhaps you are at a place where your finances are strained or you or someone close to you has been hurt physically or emotionally. Perhaps fear for your future or shame about your past cloud your thoughts, and hope seems dim. You may be wondering why you're here and what is the purpose for your life. The number one lesson of this book is: stop and pull up to the intersection where all of who you are can intersect with all of who God is. Allow your weaknesses, fears, and any other daunting obstacles in your life to connect with the God who is the source of wisdom, omnipotent power, the God whose name is love, and let Him show you the way to victory!

Chapter 16: Study Questions

The Bible says the Father holds our times and our seasons (Acts 1:7). Do you have a hard time trusting God with the direction for your life?

What season of life are you in? Is it a time of sowing through prayer or through actions such as giving of your time, studying, or working extra hard on a particular endeavor? Or is it a time for reaping the fruit of your labors? Have you prayed about the season you're in?

Is the Holy Spirit speaking to you of next steps? Are there things you must do to prepare spiritually, emotionally and physically?

To contact the author:

*Ms. Johnson can be reached through Life Change
International, whose website is: Lifechangeintl.com.*

or call
Hope Christian Church, Bowie, MD
1-800-327-2724